The
Nature
of Spiritual
Growth

The Nature of Spiritual Growth

JOHN WESLEY

BETHANY HOUSE PUBLISHERS
MINNEAPOLIS, MINNESOTA 55438
A Division of Bethany Fellowship, Inc.

Formerly entitled *The Holy Spirit and Power*.

Published by Bethany House Publishers
A Division of Bethany Fellowship, Inc.
6820 Auto Club Road, Minneapolis, Minnesota 55438

Printed in the United States of America

Library of Congress Cataloging-in-Publication Data

Weakley, Clare G.
      The nature of spiritual growth.

      (The Wesley library for today's reader)
      Previously published as: The Holy Spirit and power.
      "A modern translation of ten of John Wesley's 'Standard sermons' as they relate to the Holy Spirit and His works"—Pref.
      Bibliography: p.
      1. Holy Spirit—Sermons. 2. Sermons, English.
I. Wesley, John, 1703-1791. Sermons on several occasions. Selections.
II. Title. III. Series: Wesley, John, 1703-1791. Wesley library for today's reader.
BT122.W43   1986   231'.3   86-6811
ISBN 0-87123-876-4 (pbk.)

JOHN WESLEY (1703–1791) was the founder of Methodism. Although raised in a godly home and trained for the ministry at Oxford, Wesley's failure as a missionary to the colonists and Indians in Georgia (1735–1738) revealed his unsaved condition. Strongly influenced upon his return to England by the Moravian Peter Boehler, Wesley was converted (May 1738) to genuine faith in Christ while reading Luther's preface to Romans.

Shortly after his conversion, Wesley visited the Moravian settlement at Herrnhut and met Count Zinzendorf. He returned to England and embarked on his lifework. His objective was "to reform the nation, particularly the Church, and to spread Scriptural holiness over the land." He declared that he had only "one point of view—to promote so far as I am able vital, practical religion; and by the grace of God to beget, preserve, and increase the life of God in the souls of men." Some have viewed him as the eighteenth-century apostle commissioned to evangelize Great Britain.

Wesley discovered the most effective medium for reaching the masses was open-air preaching and his life became one of an itinerant preacher. Facing the Church's resistance to his evangelical doctrine, Wesley formed societies in the wake of his mission. The organization of Methodism was thus a direct outcome of his success in preaching the gospel. Wesley's writings include his now classic *Journals*, sermons, letters, expositions, tracts, histories, and abridgments.

CLARE WEAKLEY, JR. is a businessman, lecturer, and chaplain-at-large in his community. He received a B.A. from Southern Methodist University, and an M.A. from Perkins Seminary. He is married and he and his family make their home in Dallas.

Contents

Preface

John Wesley is becoming one of the most talked about theologians of our time. He is the spiritual father of more than thirty-five denominations, the largest being The United Methodist Church, and also the spiritual grandfather of millions of members of The Salvation Army, The Church of the Nazarene, and Pentecostal, Full Gospel, Holiness, and Charismatic renewal groups. Most of these are fully aware of their relationship to Wesley and his eighteenth century "Methodist" revival. The result is that many Christians regularly refer to Wesley's ideas, sermons, and spiritual experiences.

John Wesley's unique and apostolic mission is properly valued by those who have studied his life. His intense need to record almost everything he said or did has been a blessing to subsequent generations. The entire text of his adult *Journal* exists. In addition, many of his sermons and letters are still in print.

In spite of the existence of these important works, many have been out of general circulation for years. The limited use of his writings may be due to his eighteenth century style, vocabulary, and syntax. Whatever the reason, few have studied his basic writings directly. Most have relied upon the studies of a few scholars and ministers for their Wesleyan information. The result is that Christians have only heard about John Wesley. They have not heard him speak directly to them. His magnificent "Standard Sermons" have remained dust collectors on library shelves.

In recent years, new literary trends have opened the Bible to vernacular translations. The modern Christian has overwhelmingly endorsed this type of translation. He believes faithful translation of thoughts and ideas has priority over literal translation of words. The result is the

Bible has been opened to many who could not or would not read the more literal translations.

Public acceptance of these modern translations has made this book possible. Old traditions no longer limit us to verbatim translations of Wesley's works. We can now use our contemporary vocabulary to translate John Wesley's sermons into modern English. Now, every person who is seeking fresh understanding of the living Christian faith can read Wesley's work. It is no longer necessary to be satisfied with secondhand statements about Wesley and what he said about his faith.

This would have pleased John Wesley. He made a great effort to speak in the language of the masses. In the introduction to his published sermons, paragraphs two and three, he announced this intent. The two paragraphs quoted below describe the intent of his sermon style.

But I am throughly sensible; these are not proposed in such a manner as some may expect. Nothing here appears in an elaborate, elegant, or oratorical dress. If it had been my desire or design to write thus, my leisure would not permit. But, in truth, I, at present, designed nothing less; for I now write, as I generally speak, *ad populum*—to the bulk of mankind, to those who neither relish nor understand the art of speaking; but who, notwithstanding, are competent judges of those truths which are necessary to present and future happiness. I mention this, that curious readers may spare themselves the labour of seeking for what they will not find.

I design plain truth for plain people. Therefore, of set purpose, I abstain from all nice and philosophical speculations; from all perplexed and intricate reasonings; and, as far as possible, from even the show of learning, unless in sometimes citing the original Scripture. I labour to avoid all words which are not easy to be understood, all which are not used in common life, and, in particular, those kinds of technical terms that so frequently occur in Bodies of Divinity; those modes of speaking which men of reading are intimately acquainted with, but which to common people are an unknown tongue. Yet, I am not assured, that I do not sometimes slide into them unawares; it is so extremely natural to imagine that a word which is familiar to ourselves is so to all the world.

This book is a modern translation of ten of John Wesley's "Standard Sermons" as they relate to the Holy Spirit and His work. Included is the last one-third of Charles Wesley's "Standard Sermon," number III, "Awake, Thou That Sleepeth," which is inserted as the prologue. These portions of this book are considered doctrinal standards for all Methodists. Also included are parts of John Wesley's testimony as chapter 1. That material is directly from its autobiographical source, *The Journal of the Rev. John Wesley*. Chapters 7 and 13 are from Wesley's letter to Dr. Conyers Middleton, which was written for publication. That letter expressed his views on the supernatural gifts of the Holy Spirit and the nature of true Christianity.

What remains to be told is the particular method used here in stringing these pearls together. The first and most obvious requirement was to chop Wesley's complex, paragraph-length sentences into simple sentences. Next, modern words were substituted for his outdated words and syntax. Redundant sentences were excluded. Finally, the material was tightened by removing sections which seemed to be personal comments not germane to the subject.

The resulting interpretation has as its core the "Standard Sermons," the recognized doctrinal base of Wesleyan theology. According to his introduction to those sermons, they include doctrines which he "usually preached."

Unfortunately, Wesley did not sort his sermons on the Holy Spirit into a particular order of progression. Thus, many of them stand as separate theological essays. Therefore it must be said that the order which is used in this book does constitute an interpretative presentation.

It is hoped that the reading of this book will open up the Wesleys to the reader. Their works can be purchased and studied in their eighteenth century form. Sections of his sermons, letters, and journal are published by The Epworth Press, London, and may be ordered through any bookstore.

Credit for preparation, editing, and encouragement on this book goes to Virginia Crews, June Bicking, and my wife, Jean. Each contributed many hours of concern and effort in the preparation of the completed manuscript. Their prayers for the will of the Holy Spirit in this endeavor had much to do with its completion.

Prologue

"Christ shall give you light."[1] Consider what an encouraging promise this is! Whoever you are, when you obey Jesus' call, He will give you His light. You cannot seek Him in vain! If you will spiritually awake and arise, He has bound himself to "give you light."

Jesus shall give you grace and glory. He will give you the light of His grace here, and the light of His glory in eternity.

God, who commanded the light to shine out of darkness, shall shine in your heart. He will give you the knowledge of His glory in the face of Jesus Christ.

On the day you come to fear the Lord, you shall receive your healing and the light and the glory of the Lord rising up in you. For on that day Jesus shall reveal himself in you, and He is the true light.

God is light, and He will give himself to every awakened sinner who waits for Him. When He comes, Jesus will dwell in your heart by faith and you shall be a temple of the living God.

Then you will be rooted and grounded in love. Along with all the saints, you will understand that which passes all worldly knowledge. You will then comprehend the breadth, length, depth, and height of that love of Jesus which is greater than knowledge.

This is man's calling. We are called to be an habitation of God through His Holy Spirit. Through His Holy Spirit dwelling in us, we are to be saints here, and partakers of the inheritance of the saints in light.

Great are these promises which are actually given to us who believe. By faith we receive the Holy Spirit which is of God to replace that spirit of the world which is in us. The sum of all the promises is that we may know the things that are freely given to us by God.

11

This Holy Spirit—Christ in us—is that great gift which, at various times and in various manners, God has promised to man. He has now fully given that gift since the time Jesus was glorified. These promises made in ancient times have now been fulfilled: "I will put my spirit within you, and cause you to walk in my statutes."[2] "I will pour my Spirit upon your descendants, and my blessing on your offspring."[3]

You can be a living witness of those things—the remission of sins and the gift of the Holy Spirit—if you believe that all things are possible to him who believes.

I ask you, in the name of Jesus, do you believe that God is still able to save? Do you believe that He is the same yesterday, today, and forever? Do you believe that He now has power on earth to forgive sins? Or do you believe that times have changed and His arm is shortened?

If you believe that He is the same today as yesterday, be of good cheer. Your sins are forgiven. God, for Jesus' sake, has forgiven you. Receive this, not as my word, but as the true word of God.

You are saved and justified freely through faith. Also, you shall be completely purified through faith which is in Jesus. You shall be assured and sealed by God that you have been given eternal life, and this life is in His Son Jesus.

Let me write freely to you. Accept this word of exhortation from me, one of the least. Your conscience bears you witness in the Holy Spirit that these statements are true if you know the Lord. Eternal life is to know God and Jesus Christ whom He sent. This experiential knowledge, and this alone, is true Christianity.

He is a Christian who has received the Spirit of Christ, the Holy Spirit. He is not a Christian if he has not received Him. It is not possible to have received Him and not know it! It is written, "In that day, you will know that I am in my Father, and you in me, and I in you."[4] This is that "Spirit of truth, whom the world cannot receive, because it neither sees him nor knows him; you know him, for he dwells with you, and will be in you."[5]

The world cannot receive Him, but utterly rejects this great promise of God with blaspheming. But every spirit which does not confess this is not of God. Such a spirit is of the antichrist who denies the inspiration of the Holy Spirit. The antichrist denies the indwelling Holy Spirit is the privilege of all believers. The antichrist denies this blessing of the gospel, this unspeakable gift, this universal promise, and this criterion of a real Christian.

Some will condition their objections. But it does not help the antichrist to say, "I do not deny the assistance of God's Spirit. I only object to this inspiration, this receiving the Holy Spirit, and being aware of Him. I only object to this feeling of the Holy Spirit, and this being moved by the Spirit, or being filled with Him. I deny these have any place in sound religion."

In denying only these, you deny the whole truth, promise, and testimony of God. The historical church knows nothing of this devilish distinction of the work of the Holy Spirit. It plainly speaks of feeling the Spirit of Christ; of being moved by the Holy Spirit, and knowing and feeling there is no other name than that of Jesus, whereby we can receive life and salvation. The church teaches us all to pray for the inspiration of the Holy Spirit. We are taught to pray that we may be filled with the Holy Spirit. Every presbyter of the church claims to have received the Holy Spirit by the laying on of hands at ordination. Therefore, to deny any of these is, in effect, to renounce the whole Christian revelation.

We need not wonder about this when we realize that the wisdom of God was always foolishness to men. So we need not wonder that the gospel mysteries continue to be hidden from the wise and prudent in our time.

As of old, this belief in the Holy Spirit is almost universally denied, ridiculed, and exploded as mere frenzy or fad. Those who believe it are still branded as madmen and fanatics.[6]

This is that falling away which was to come. It is that great apostasy of all orders and degrees of men, which we find has spread over the earth. "Run to and fro in the streets of Jerusalem, and see if you can find a man," a man who loves God with all his heart, and serves Him will all his strength.

See how our own country mourns and suffers under the outpourings and overflowings of ungodliness! What crimes of every kind are committed each day, too often with impunity. Many sin with a high-handedness and glory in their shame! They brag about their acts. Who can count up all the oaths, curses, profanities, blasphemies; all the Sabbath-breaking, gluttony, drunkenness, revenge; the fornications, adulteries, and various uncleannesses; the frauds, injustice, oppression, and extortion which cover over our land as a flood of evil?

And even those who have kept themselves away from these grosser acts are not innocent. How much anger, pride, sloth, idleness, softness, effeminacy, self-indulgence, covetousness, ambition, thirst of praise, love of the world, and fear of man is to be found among us?

How little true religion is there! Where is he who loves either God or his neighbor as Jesus has commanded?

On the one hand, there are those who have not so much as the form of godliness. On the other hand, there are those who have the form only. One is the open sepulcher, the other is the painted sepulcher. In any public gathering, including our own churches, one part is Sadducees and the other Pharisees. One part has almost as little concern about religion as if there were no resurrection. The other part makes religion a mere lifeless form, a dull round of external performances, without true faith, the love of God, or joy in the Holy Spirit.

I wish to God that I could exclude all of us from this charge. My heart's desire and prayer for you is that you may be saved from this overflowing of ungodliness, and excluded from this group. But are you excluded? God knows, and our own consciences know otherwise. You have not kept yourselves pure. You are also corrupt and abominable. There are but few who understand God and worship Him in spirit and truth.

We are a generation that has not set our hearts right. Our spirits do not cling steadfastly unto God. He has called and appointed us to be the salt of the earth. "But if salt has lost its taste, how shall its saltiness be restored? It is no longer good for anything except to be thrown out and trodden under foot by men."[7]

"Shall I not visit you for these things?" says the Lord. "Shall not my soul be avenged on such a nation as this?" We do not know how soon He may say to the sword, "Sword, go through this land." He has given us a long time to repent. He lets us alone this year also. But He warns and awakens us by thunder. His judgments are abroad in this world. He judges all of us. We have all the reason to expect the worst. He could come quickly and remove us from our special place unless we repent and do the first works, and return to the principles of the living faith, truth, and simplicity of the gospel.

Perhaps we are now resisting the last effort of divine grace to save us. Perhaps we have almost filled up the cup with our iniquities, by rejecting the counsel of God against ourselves, and casting out His messengers.

It is high time for us to awake out of spiritual sleep before the great trumpet of the Lord is blown, and our land becomes a field of blood.

O God, in the midst of wrath, remember mercy! Be glorified in our reformation, not in our destruction! Let us hear your rod and you who appointed it. Now that your judgments are abroad in the earth, let the inhabitants of the world learn your righteousness! Turn us, O good Lord, and let your anger cease from us. O Lord, look down from heaven, behold and visit this vine, and cause us to know the time of our visitation. Help us, O God of our salvation, for the glory of your name! O deliver us, and be merciful to our sins, for your name's sake, and so we will not go back from you. O let us live, and we shall call upon your name. Turn us again, O Lord God of Hosts! Show the light of your countenance, and we shall be whole.

Now unto Him who is able to do exceeding abundantly above all that we can ask or think, according to the power that works in us, unto Him be glory in the church by Christ Jesus throughout all ages, world without end! Amen.

CHARLES WESLEY

From Charles Wesley, "Awake Thou That Sleepest," John Wesley, *Forty-Four Sermons* (London: The Epworth Press, 1944), Sermon III, pt. III.

1

Finding Faith

Many comforters assured me that I had faith.[1] As a Wesley, I was supposed to have faith. I was an ordained minister from a family of ministers. My brother, father, grandfathers, and a great-grandfather were all ministers. I was ordained at the age of twenty-two.[2] I received my Master of Arts degree from Oxford, England. I preached on faith to the faculty and students at St. Mary's Church, Oxford.[3] But I did not have the faith which I wanted and knew that I needed. This faith by the power of the Holy Spirit would come to me later. Then I would be able to lead many into the same powerful spiritual experience.

I had a sort of faith during my early life. But devils also have a sort of faith. Still, neither they nor I received the faith of the covenant of promise. Even the apostles had a sort of faith when they were first with Jesus in Cana. Then and there, they "believed on him" in a way. But they did not yet have the faith which overcomes the world.

The faith I wanted was a sure trust and confidence in God. I wanted to experience forgiveness from my sins and a oneness with God through the work of Jesus. I wanted to be

17

returned to God through the faith Paul wrote about, especially in his letter to the Romans. Like him, I wanted a faith which would enable me to say, "It is no longer I who live, but Christ who lives in me; and the life I now live in the flesh I live by faith in the Son of God, who loved me and gave himself for me."

I wanted a faith which no one can have without knowing he has it. Many imagine they have this type of faith, but do not. My comforters imagined I had it, but I did not. I remained miserable in their poor comfort.

Everyone possessing this true faith is free from sin. The whole body of sin in him is destroyed. He is free from fear, receiving peace through Jesus while rejoicing in hope of the glory of God. He is free from doubt, having the love of God shed abroad in his heart through the Holy Spirit which is given to him. He is assured that he is truly a child of God through the witness which the Holy Spirit bears in the heart of the faithful.[4]

Having preached about this true faith, I was sure of its substance. I knew that I was yet to attain such a faith.

In order to find this faith, I contracted to serve as a missionary. I was not searching for any financial gain in missionary work. God had given me many material blessings already. I was not seeking any honor. Purely and simply, I was seeking to live wholly to the glory of God and to save my own soul.[5]

By God's grace, I was able to have direct witness of this living faith through a group of Germans soon after leaving for the mission field. There were twenty-six of these unusual Christians on the ship.[6]

In mid-ocean, we encountered three violent storms in rapid succession. All the passengers, except these Germans, were in fear for their lives. I had to ask myself, since I was so unwilling to die, "How is it that I have no faith?"[7]

The third storm—a hurricane—hit at noon on Sunday. By four it was more violent than any of the other storms. The winds roared and whistled all around us. The ship rocked to and fro with great violence. It shook and jarred with an unequal, grating motion, so that no one could stand without holding on. Shocks came every ten minutes. It seemed as if those shocks would tear the ship apart.

At seven I made my way into the quarters of the Germans. I had already observed the seriousness of their behavior. They gave continual proof of their humility. They were willing to do the most servile tasks rejected by others, and take no pay. They would say of the tasks performed, "It was good for their proud hearts." And also, "Their loving Savior had done more for them."

Every day was another occasion of showing a meekness which no affront or insult could remove. If they were mistreated, they went away without a complaint.

I wanted to see if they had been freed from fear. I knew they were delivered from pride, anger, and revenge. But what about fear?

They began their services with a psalm. In the middle of it, a great wave rolled over the ship. It covered the deck and poured down inside as if the ship were about to sink. A terrible scream came from the other passengers, but the Germans calmly sang on. I asked one of them afterwards, "Were you not afraid?"

He answered, "I thank God I was not."

"But were your women and children afraid?"

"No. Our women and children are not afraid to die," he replied mildly.

After that I tried to watch their behavior as often as possible. They were always busy, usefully employed, cheerful, and in good humor. They had done away with all strife, anger, bitterness, clamor, and evil-speaking. They walked and lived as true witnesses of Christ.[8]

A contrast to their meekness was the impression which I gave to some. One man was particularly cold toward me. I asked him the reason for this. He gave me a detailed reply.

"I like nothing you do. All your sermons are satires upon particular persons; therefore, I will never hear you again; and all the people are of the same mind, for we won't hear ourselves abused.

"Besides, they say they are Protestants. But as for you, they cannot tell of what religion you are. They never heard such a religion before. They do not know what to make of it. And your private behavior: All the quarrels that have been here since you came, have been 'long of you.' Indeed, there is neither man nor woman in the town who minds a word you say. And so you may preach long enough, but nobody will come to hear you."[9]

After two years of poor results in this chosen work, I thought it was time to leave the mission field. I took a ship home.[10] On the return, I had much private time to think about my Christianity. Had this solitude helped me to become more Christian? Not if Jesus Christ is the model of Christianity![11]

My mind was full of thoughts. Some I wrote in my journal. I became a missionary to convert the heathens; but oh, who shall convert me? Who, what, is He who will deliver me from this evil heart of unbelief? I have a fair summer religion. I can talk well, and believe myself while no danger is near. But let death look me in the face, and my spirit is troubled.[12]

Then on the last evening aboard ship, I wrote this review of my situation. "It is now two years and almost four months since I left my native country in order to teach heathens the nature of Christianity. But what have I learned myself in the meantime? Why, what I the least of all suspected! I went to the mission field to convert others, but was never myself converted to God. I am not mad, though I thus speak, but I speak the words of truth and soberness; if haply some of those who still dream may awake and see, that as I am, so are they.

"Are they students of philosophy? So was I. In ancient or modern languages? So was I, also. Are they informed in the field of theology? I, too, have studied it for many years. Can they talk fluently about spiritual things? I could do the very same thing. Are they generous in their giving alms? I gave all that I had to feed the poor. Do they give of their time as well as of their money? I have labored more than them all. Are they willing to suffer for others? I have given up my friends, reputation, comfort, and country. I have put my life at stake wandering in strange lands. I have risked my life at sea, been parched with heat, consumed by work and weariness, or whatever it pleased God to allow upon me.

"But does all this make me more acceptable to God? Does all I ever did or can know, say, give, do, or suffer justify me in His sight? By no means! If the words of God are true, all these things, though holy, just, and good when enobled by faith in Christ, are waste without such faith, good only to be purged away by the fire that shall never be quenched.

"This is what I have learned in my travels and services. I am fallen short of the glory of God. My whole heart is altogether corrupt and abominable. As a result, my whole life cannot produce good fruit because I am an evil tree. I am alienated from the life of God as a child of wrath, an heir of hell. My own works, my own sufferings, my own righteousness are far from reconciling me to God whom I have offended. These make no atonement for the least of my sins, and my sins are more numerous than the hairs on my head. I know in my heart there is nothing in or of myself which can plead an earning of God's mercy. I have no hope except of being justified—saved freely through the redemption that is in Jesus alone.[13]

"My only hope is that if I seek Jesus, I shall find Christ. Then I shall "be found in him, not having a righteousness of my own, based on law, but that which is through faith in Christ, the righteousness from God that depends on faith."[14] [15]

There are many reasons to thank God for the missionary work, even though my plans were not fulfilled. By this experience, He had humbled me and shown me what was truly in my heart. I learned to be more cautious about men. I am now sure that if we trust God in all our ways, He will surely direct our paths in this world. One side effect was that I became free from my fear of the sea, a fear troubling me since my youth.

And equally important, I was able to meet and know many of his true servants. During this time, I learned the languages of German, Spanish and Italian. I believed some good use would come of this in the future.[16]

Within a week of my return home, God sent three more German Christians who had the faith which I sought.[17] One of them, Peter Bohler, was to lead both my brother Charles and me into this new faith. I was able to spend much time with Peter.[18]

With regard to my own life, I wrote down and renewed all the resolutions of my life.

1. I would use absolute openness and unreserve in all my conversation.

2. I would continually seek to be serious, not willingly participating in levity or laughter even for a moment.

3. I would never speak unless it tended to the glory of God. In particular, I would not talk of worldly things. Others may, some must. That would be of no concern to me.

4. I would engage in no activity for pleasure unless it tended to the glory of God. I wanted to thank God at all times

for all things. Therefore, I must reject all activities which I believe I could not so thank Him in and for.[19]

In my discussion with Peter Bohler, I was amazed by his accounts of a living faith. He insisted that the fruits of holiness and happiness were part of such a faith. I went back to my Greek New Testament to verify his claims. I resolved to accept the testimony of the Scriptures. I was sure that God would direct my search. He would show me whether this doctrine was of Him.[20]

Even though I did not yet have this living faith, I began to speak about it in public.[21] I went into the prison to preach to the condemned. I prayed with a condemned man. He knelt down with much heaviness and confusion. He arose in cheerfulness.

"I am now ready to die. I know Christ has taken away my sins. There is no more condemnation for me," he eagerly reported. As he was taken to his execution, he continued in the same composed cheerfulness. In his last moments he was the same. He enjoyed perfect peace, assured that he was accepted in Jesus.[22]

On my next visit with Peter, I assured him I had no objections about his claims on the nature of faith. I agreed that faith is a sure trust and confidence which man has in God, that through the merits of Christ his sins are forgiven, and he is reconciled to God. I could not deny that both holiness and happiness were fruits of the living faith, just as he claimed. My review of the Scriptures proved this.

What I could not understand was what he spoke of as an instantaneous work. I could not understand how this faith could be given in a moment. How could one be turned from sin and misery into righteousness and joy in the Holy Spirit instantaneously?

I returned to the Scriptures to search this point again. I particularly studied the Acts of the Apostles. To my utter astonishment, I found scarcely any instances of conversions except the instantaneous kind. Few were as slow as that of Paul who was three days in the labor of the new birth. I had but one retreat left. I granted God did these things in the first age of Christianity, but times had changed. Was there any reason to believe that God works in the same way now as He did then?

The next day I was beaten out of this retreat, also. Peter brought me Christians who testified God had changed them in a moment. In a moment, they said, God had given them a living faith in Jesus. That faith transferred them from darkness into light, out of sin and fear into holiness and happiness.

Here my disputing ended. I could now only cry out, "Lord, help my unbelief!"[23]

My brother Charles was greatly opposed to my understanding of the living faith. It made him angry to hear me say that I did not have real faith. He called this "the new faith."[24] However, Charles agreed to a long conversation with Peter about it. It pleased God to open Charles's eyes. He also saw clearly what was the nature of the one true living faith. Through grace alone, we are saved.[25]

Charles experienced this new living faith before I did. He was staying with a friend while sick with pleurisy. Because he was too sick to go out, several of us visited him on Sunday morning, May 21. It was Whitsunday—Pentecost Sunday. We prayed with him and left for church. Later that day, the Holy Spirit healed him and gave him the living faith in a moment.[26]

I had continued to seek this faith, though with some strange indifference, dullness, and coldness until May 24. In the evening of that day, I went very unwillingly to a prayer meeting in Aldersgate Street. About 8:45, I was listening to a reading of Luther's preface to the Epistle to the Romans. While he was describing the change which God works in the heart through faith in Christ, I felt my heart strangely warmed. I felt that I did trust in Christ, Christ alone, for salvation. An assurance was given me that He had taken away my sins, even mine, and saved me from the law of sin and death.[27]

The moment I awakened the next morning, the love of Jesus, my Master, was in my heart and in my mouth. All my strength came from keeping my eyes fixed upon Him, and my soul waiting on Him continually. In church in the afternoon, I could taste the good word of God in the anthem. Its first line was, "My song shall be always of the loving-kindness of the Lord; with my mouth will I ever be showing forth your truth from one generation to another."

Yet Satan injected a fear into me. "If you do believe, why do you not feel a greater change?"

"That I do not know. But this I know, I have now peace with God. And I do not sin today. Jesus, my Master, has forbidden me to take any thought about tomorrow." This answer came from something deep within me. It was not me.

"But is not any sort of fear," continued the tempter, "a proof that you do not believe?"

I wanted Jesus to answer for me. I opened the Bible and my eyes fell upon the words of St. Paul. "Without were fightings, within were fears." This inferred that I well may have some fears within me, but I must go on treading them under my feet.[28]

On the following Sunday, I waked in peace, but not in joy. I remained in the same quiet state until evening. Then came the first persecution for my new faith. Many such persecutions were to follow over the years. I was roughly attacked in a large group as a fanatic, seducer, and a setter-forth of new doctrines. By the blessing of God, I was not moved to anger. After a calm and short reply, I went away. I had preached in two churches that day. It was the last time I would be allowed to preach at either. I continued to be concerned for those who were seeking death through error in their lives.[29]

It was my wish to visit the Germans. I wanted to be with the main body of Christians from which Peter and those whom I met on board the ship came. I was able to spend two months there. Some of this time was spent with Peter's family.[30]

In Germany, I continually met with living proofs of the power of faith. Many persons there had been saved from inward as well as outward sin by the love of God in their hearts. They were freed from all doubt and fear by the abiding witness of the Holy Spirit who had been given them.[31]

I heard their senior minister preach on four occasions. Each time his topic was one which I wanted to hear. Three of these sermons concerned those who are weak in faith, the ones who are saved—justified—but have not yet received the new, clean heart. They have received forgiveness through the blood of Christ, but have not received the constant indwelling of the Holy Spirit.[32]

After returning from Germany, I began to declare this good news of experienced salvation. I preached as often as three times a day. I preached in the prisons to the convicted and the condemned.[33]

One day I saw a woman who was raving mad, screaming and tormenting herself continually. I had a strong desire to speak to her. The moment I began she became still. Tears ran down her cheeks all the time I was telling her, "Jesus of Nazareth is able and willing to deliver you."[34]

Those who had received this new living faith through the Holy Spirit continued to meet together. About sixty of us were holding a love feast on New Year's Eve on Fetter

Lane. At about three in the morning, as we were continuing in prayer, the power of God came mightily upon us. Many cried out in complete joy. Others were knocked to the ground. As soon as we recovered a little from that awe and amazement at God's presence, we broke out in praise. "We praise you, O God; we acknowledge you to be the Lord."[35]

The Holy Spirit began to move among us with amazing power when we met in His name. One of the most surprising instances of His power which I ever saw happened to one of the opposers. I was visiting a woman who was furious about this new faith, and zealous in opposing it. My arguments only increased her anger. I broke off the dispute and asked her to join me in prayer. She agreed and we knelt together. In a few minutes she fell over in extreme agony, both in body and soul. Soon after she cried out with great earnestness, "Now I know I am forgiven for Christ's sake."[36]

A few days later I visited her again. Gathered that evening were some of her neighbors who also objected to the new faith. One man was attempting to pervert this truth. I entered into the controversy to speak on both the cause and effects of salvation. During the dispute, a woman listener fell pierced as with a sword. She left to go to another house, but began crying out while still in the street. As soon as we prayed for her forgiveness, He sent her that assurance.[37]

These unusual works of the Holy Spirit continued to follow and bless my ministry.

At Baldwin Street, I preached on the fourth chapter of Acts. Then I asked God to confirm this teaching. Immediately one who was standing there cried out aloud as though she were in the agonies of death. As surprised as I was, I was able to continue in prayer. We prayed until she received her sense of forgiveness and could give thanks to God. Soon after that, two other persons were seized with strong pain. It was not long before they likewise burst forth into praises of God, their Savior. Finally, a stranger was overwhelmed with both joy and love. He had received forgiveness of backsliding.[38]

At another place a young man was seized with a violent trembling all over. In a few minutes his heart was filled with sorrow, and he sank to the ground. We continued in prayer until God raised him up. He was then full of peace and joy in the Holy Spirit.[39]

Later, while preaching in prison, I felt called to say that God wills all men to receive this saving faith. I called to God to bear witness to this truth. Immediately one, and another, and another sunk to the ground. People dropped on every side as thunderstruck. One of them cried aloud. We prayed to God on her behalf, and He gave her the joy of the Holy Spirit. The same occurred with a second woman. Our prayers were answered and He gave her the peace of the Holy Spirit.[40]

The next day the whole prison was filled with the cries of those whose hearts were being touched by God. Two of these received joy in a moment to the astonishment of the onlookers.[41]

We knew many were offended by the cries of those on whom the power of God came. One so offended was a physician who was afraid these cases involved either fraud or mistake. In one of my services, he stood next to an acquaintance of many years. His acquaintance broke out into strong cries and tears. The physician could hardly believe his own eyes and ears. He stood close to observe every symptom. Great drops of sweat ran down her face and all her bones shook. He did not know what to think, being convinced it was neither fraud nor any natural disorder. When both her body and soul were healed in a moment, he admitted it to be the work of God.[42]

Many continued to be offended, even more than before.

Later at Baldwin Street my voice could hardly be heard due to the groanings and cries of those calling to God to save. A Quaker stood by very displeased at the confusion. He was biting his lips and knitting his brows. Suddenly he went down as thunderstruck. He appeared to be in terrible agony. We prayed to God to forgive him of his mistake. Soon he lifted his head and cried aloud, "Now I know you are a prophet of the Lord."[43]

Similar experiences continued to increase as I preached. It seemed prudent to preach and write on the work of the Holy Spirit.[44] Many of these sermons were published. The published sermons include the doctrines which I usually preached. All of the following sermons are from those basic doctrines.[45]

2

The Way to God

*The kingdom of God is at hand; repent, and believe in the
gospel. (Mark 1:15)*

The meaning of the words above needs to be pondered.
First, the kingdom of God, which Jesus says is at hand, is the
nature of true religion. Second is the way into it, through
repentance and belief in the gospel.

Our first consideration is the nature of true religion, called
the kingdom of God by Jesus in this Scripture. The same
expression was used by Paul in his letter to the Romans.
There Paul explained this by writing, "The kingdom of God
is not meat and drink; but righteousness, and peace, and joy
in the Holy Ghost."[1]

The kingdom of God, or true religion, is not meat and
drink. It is well known that many have been zealous in the
keeping of the ceremonial law of Moses.[2] Not only did the
unconverted Jews do this, but also large numbers of the
early Christians. They observed all rules found in the Old
Testament either concerning meat and drink offerings, or
the distinction between clean and unclean meats. They not

31

only observed the rules themselves, but forced the same rules on all new Christians as they turned to God. Some of these even taught, "Except ye be circumcised after the manner of Moses, ye cannot be saved."[3]

Objecting to this, Paul declared here and in other places that true religion does not consist of meat and drink or any ritual observances. Indeed, it does not lie in any outward thing whatever. It is not in anything outside of the heart. The whole essence of true religion is in righteousness, peace, and joy in the Holy Spirit.

Forms and ceremonies, even of the best kind, are outward things, and not true religion. Suppose these religious ceremonies to be decent, significant, expressive or spiritual things, and helpful to both the educated and the uneducated. Consider them, as in the case of the Jews, to be appointed by God himself. Nevertheless, they do not contain true religion even during the time that God's appointment of them remains in force. Strictly speaking, they do not contain true religion at all. This is even more true regarding rites and forms that are only creations of men.

The religion of Jesus rises infinitely higher and goes immensely deeper than all of these ceremonies. Ceremonies are good in their place, just as long as they are subservient to true religion. It is not necessary to object to them if they are used only as occasional helps to human weakness. But let no one carry them any further. Let no one dream that rituals have any intrinsic worth. Never believe that religion cannot exist without rituals. Such a belief would make any ritual an abomination to the Lord.

The nature of religion does not properly consist of outward actions of any kind. It cannot be said to rest in forms of worship, rites and ceremonies. It is true that a man cannot have religion and at the same time be guilty of vicious immoral actions. Neither does he have religion who does to others what he would not have others do to him if he were in the same circumstances. And it is also true that he can have no real religion if he knows how to do good and does not do it. Yet a man may both abstain from outward evil and do good, and still have no religion. Further, two persons may do the same good outward act—as feeding of the hungry—and one be religious, while the other is not. This is because one may do the act out of love and the other for the love of praise. Although real religion leads to good works and words, its real nature still lies deeper. Real religion lies in the hidden heart of man.

I say of the heart, because religion does not consist of right opinions or orthodoxy. While such matters are not necessarily outward things, they are not of the heart, but of the understanding. A person may be orthodox in every point, espousing right opinions and zealously defending them; he may think correctly concerning the Trinity, and every other approved doctrine taken from the Scriptures; he may agree with all of the historical creeds, and yet have no religion at all. He may be as orthodox as the devil, and still have no more religion than a pagan. He is indeed a pagan if he is a stranger to the religion of the heart.

This alone is religion as it is truly so-called. This alone is of value in the sight of God. Paul summarized religion in three particulars: righteousness, peace, and joy in the Holy Spirit.

The first of these is righteousness. We cannot be confused about this if we remember the words of Jesus. He described the two great branches of it upon which hang all of the law and the prophets.

The first branch is the first and great commandment: "You shall love the Lord your God with all your heart, and will all your soul, and with all your mind, and with all your strength."[4]

You shall delight yourself in the Lord your God. You shall

seek and find all happiness in Him. He shall be your shield and exceeding glad reward in time and eternity. All of your bones shall say, "Whom have I in heaven but you? And there is none upon earth that I desire besides you."

You shall hear and fulfill His word, who said, "My son, give me your heart." And having given Him your heart, your inmost soul, to reign there without a rival, you may well cry out, in the fullness of your heart, "I love thee, O LORD, my strength. The LORD is my rock, and my fortress, and my deliverer, my God, my rock, in whom I take refuge, my shield, and the horn of my salvation, my stronghold."[5]

The second great commandment is similar to the first, and is the second great branch of Christian righteousness. "You shall love your neighbor as yourself." You shall love! You shall embrace him with the most tender goodwill, the most inflamed desires of preventing or removing all evil from him and of obtaining for him every possible good.

Your neighbor is not only your friend, your kinsman, or your acquaintance. Your neighbor is not only he who is virtuous, friendly, and loving toward you. Your neighbor is every human, every soul which God has made.

The word neighbor does not exclude those whom you have never seen and whom you do not know—either by face or name—or those whom you know to be evil and unthankful. Even those who despitefully use you and persecute you are not excluded. You shall love them all as you love yourself. You shall thirst after their happiness with the same thirst you have for your own. You shall use the same unwearied care to screen them from whatever might grieve or hurt either their bodies or souls.

Now is not this love the fulfilling of the law? Is it not the whole of all Christian righteousness? Is it not the sum of all inward righteousness? Does it not necessarily imply humility of mind, gentleness, meekness, and longsuffering?

And does not outward righteousness come from inward righteousness, because love works no evil toward his neighbor, either by word or deed. Love cannot willingly hurt or grieve anyone. Love is also zealous of good works. Every lover of mankind, as he has opportunity, does good to all men. Without any partiality or hypocrisy, he is full of mercy and good fruits.

Happiness as well as holiness is implied by a heart which is right toward both God and man. True religion is not only righteousness, but also peace and joy in the Holy Spirit. What peace? The peace of God, which God only can give, and the world cannot take away. It is the peace which passes all understanding—all rational thinking. This peace is a supernatural sensation, a divine taste of the powers of the world to come.

Natural man cannot know this peace from the things of the world. He can never know it in his present state because it is divinely given and spiritually discerned. It is a peace that banishes all doubt, all painful uncertainty. It comes from the Holy Spirit bearing witness to the spirit of a Christian that he is a child of God. This peace banishes all fear, which carries with it torment. It removes the fear of the wrath of God, the fear of hell, the fear of the devil, and in particular, the fear of death. He who has the peace of God desires, according to the will of God, to depart now to be with Christ.

Joy in the Holy Spirit follows this peace of God whenever it is fixed in the soul. Joy is put in the heart by the Holy Spirit. It is the Holy Spirit who works in us that calm, humble, rejoicing in God, through Christ Jesus. It is Jesus by whom we have now received this atonement, the reconciliation with God. It is He who enables us boldly to confirm the truth of the psalmist's declaration, "Blessed [happy] is he whose transgression [unrighteousness] is forgiven, whose sin is covered."[6]

It is the Holy Spirit who inspires the Christian soul with

that even, solid joy that arises from the testimony of the Spirit that he is a child of God. It is that Spirit who allows him to rejoice with joy unspeakable, in the hope of the glory of God. This hope is of the glorious image of God, which is in part and shall be fully revealed in heaven for him, and which does not fade away.

This happiness and holiness, joined in one, are sometimes called "the kingdom of God." Jesus terms it that in the text before us. It is also referred to as the "kingdom of heaven," because it is the immediate fruit of God's work in the soul.

As soon as God sets up His throne in our hearts, we are instantly filled with this righteousness, peace, and joy in the Holy Spirit. It is called the kingdom of heaven, because it is a degree of heaven opened in our souls in this life. Whoever experiences this work of the Holy Spirit can testify in this life and the one to come: "Everlasting life is won, glory on earth has begun."[7]

The constant theme of the Scripture, to which all agree, is that God has given us eternal life, and this life is in Jesus. He who has Jesus reigning in his heart has life, everlasting life.[8] For this is life eternal, to know the only true God, and Jesus whom God has sent.[9]

This kingdom of God, or of heaven, is at hand! As these words were originally spoken by Jesus, they implied that the time was fulfilled then. God, being made manifest in the flesh, would then set up His kingdom among men and reign in the hearts of His people. And is the time now fulfilled? Jesus said, "Lo, I am with you always [you who preach the remission of sins in my name], to the close of the age."[10]

Therefore, whenever and wherever the gospel of Christ is preached, His kingdom is near at hand. It is not far from any one of us. You may enter into it at this very moment if you hear and follow His words, "Repent and believe the gospel."

And what does "repent" mean? It first means, know

yourself. It is the conviction or self-knowledge. Awake then and admit that you are a sinner. Discover what kind of a sinner you are. Know the corruption of your inner nature. It is your inner feelings that have strayed far from God's original righteousness. It is because of the corrupt inner nature that the flesh always lusts contrary to the Spirit of God. We sin through our carnal mind, which is in enmity against God and not subject to the law of God, and cannot be.

Know that you are corrupted in every power, in every faculty of your soul. Know that you are completely out of the correct course, because you are corrupted in every one of these.

The eyes of man's spiritual understanding are so blind that he cannot see God or the things of God. The clouds of this ignorance rest upon us, and cover us with the shadow of eternal death. We know nothing that we ought to know before repentance. We do not understand God, the world, or ourselves. In this state, our will is not the will of God, but away from God and all that He loves. It is subject to all kinds of evil.

Our affections are alienated from God, and scattered everywhere toward the things of the world. All our passions, desires and aversions, joys and sorrows, hopes and fears, are out of balance. This is because they are either placed on wrong objects or placed with the wrong intensity. The result is there is no spiritual soundness of the soul. From the top of the head to the soles of the feet, there is only spiritual sickness, confusion, unrest, and sin.

This is the inbred corruption of the heart, of the inmost nature. This is the evil root which cannot grow sound branches.

Unbelief comes from this. We have no concern about being in the presence of the living God. We say, "Who can know God? Who is He that I should serve Him? God doesn't want my service."

The result of this unbelief is independence. We begin to act as though we were God. Pride comes in all forms. We say, "I am rich, increasing in worth and worldly things. I do not need God. I have everything I need."

From this set of mind comes vanity. We develop a thirst for praise with covetousness and selfish ambition. Then comes the lust of the flesh, lust of the eye, and the pride of life.

Anger, hatred, malice, revenge, envy, jealousy, evil surmisings all arise from this vanity. These attitudes and foolish lusts fill us with sorrow and unhappiness. If we do not deal with these feelings, they will finally drown our souls forever.

Now what kind of fruit can grow on this kind of branch? Only bitter fruit which is continually evil. From pride comes vain boasting, contention, and the seeking and accepting of praise from men. By taking this praise, we rob God of the glory He should receive for our talents. God does not give His glory to others.

The lust of the flesh causes gluttony or drunkenness, sensuality and luxury-seeking, fornication, and uncleanness. The result is a defiling of the body which was designed to be a temple for the Holy Spirit.

We do not have enough time to discuss all the idle words we have spoken or the evil works we have done. At worst, these words and works are either wholly evil in themselves, or at best, they are words and works which are not done to the glory of God. Our actual sins are more than we are able to count or express. They are more than the hairs of our heads. Who but God can count the sands of the sea, the drops of rain, or our iniquities?

The reward of sin is death![11] This death is both earthly and eternal. The soul that sins shall die, according to the Word of

God. It shall die the second death. This is the sentence, to be punished with everlasting destruction, out of His presence. It is to be removed from the glory of His power. Every sinner is under the sentence of hellfire. He is doomed already, unhappily headed toward his execution.

All are guilty and deserve this everlasting death. It is the just reward for inward and outward wickedness. It is just that this sentence should take place now. Why can we not see this? Why are we not convinced that we deserve God's everlasting wrath and damnation for what we have done, in and to His creation, and to His creatures? Would not God be fair if He caused the earth to open up and swallow you? When God works in the heart of man, He gives a deep sense that these things are true. This is the beginning of repentance. We begin to realize that it is by His mere mercy that we are allowed to live. Because of this mercy, we are not swept away from the face of the earth.

What will you do to appease God and prevent His justifiable anger over all of your sins? What will you do to escape the punishment you know that you have earned? You can do nothing! There is nothing we can do to make amends to God for one evil act, word, or thought of our past. If, from this moment, you could begin to do all things correctly and righteously, in uninterrupted obedience and purity, even this would not pay for the past. The debt would remain as great as it ever was. The present and future obedience of all men upon earth and all angels in heaven would never make restitution for one sin.

How absurd is the thought of atoning for our own sins! How foolish it is to think that anything we can do will repay or remove them! Such work costs far more than one or all can pay. By our own efforts, there is no way to remove our guilt. Because there is no help from within, without a doubt we would be sentenced to everlasting death.

Suppose that perfect obedience could atone for past sins. This would profit you nothing, because you are not able to obey God's commandments perfectly at any one point. You cannot do it. How will you change your life from evil to good—both outward and inward? This is impossible unless the heart is changed first. So long as the tree remains evil, it cannot produce good fruit. Are you able to change your own heart from sin to holiness? Are you able to awake a soul that is dead in sin, dead to God, and alive only to worldly things? You are no more able to do this than you can raise a dead body from the grave. It cannot even be done in degrees. You cannot raise a dead body by degrees and you cannot awaken your soul by degrees. You can do nothing more or less in this endeavor. You are utterly without the strength required to change yourself.

To be deeply aware of how helpless we are is the requirement for repentance, the forerunner to the kingdom of God. An awareness of how guilty and how sinful we are is also needed. The sum of the two—guilt for sin and helplessness in sin—is repentance, which must be experienced by all children of God.

There are certain feelings which are part of this repentance. There is a remorse and self-condemnation so great that our attempts at self-justification cease. There is a shame so great that we feel we cannot face God. There is a fear of the punishment of God. There is an awareness that a curse is hanging over the heads of all those who forget God and His will. There is a fiery indignation due to all those who do not obey the instructions of Jesus.

The result is an earnest desire to escape from that indignation, to cease from evil, and to learn to do right. When this occurs, you are not far from the kingdom of God. One step more comes after repentance. One step more and you shall enter into the kingdom of God—heaven on earth.

You have repented, now believe the gospel.

The gospel is good tidings, good news for guilty, helpless sinners. In the largest sense of the word, gospel means the whole revelation made to men by Jesus Christ. This includes the whole account of what our Lord did and suffered when He lived among men. The essence of all of this is, Jesus came into the world to save sinners. The well-known summary is, "God so loved the world that he gave his only Son, that whoever believes in him should not perish but have eternal life."[12] The good news to the sinner is, "He was bruised for our iniquities; upon him was the chastisement that made us whole, and with his stripes we are healed."[13]

If you come to believe this, the kingdom of God is yours. By faith, you receive the promise. Jesus pardons and absolves all who truly repent and believe this good news. As soon as God speaks to your heart, "Be of good cheer, your sins are forgiven," His kingdom comes into you and you have righteousness, peace, and joy in the Holy Spirit.

Beware that you do not deceive yourself regarding the nature of this faith. It is not a bare assent to the truth of the Bible, the articles of creeds, or of all that is contained in the Old and New Testaments. Some have falsely believed that such is faith. The devils believe this much along with the rest of us. They believe this much and are still devils!

Over and above all this, it is a sure trust in the mercy of God, through Christ Jesus. It is a confidence in a pardoning God. It is a divine evidence or conviction that God was in Jesus, reconciling the world to himself, not imputing to them their former sins and trespasses. In particular, it is belief that Jesus has loved me and given himself for me. It is the realizing that I, even I, am now reconciled to God by the blood Jesus shed on the cross.

Do you believe this? If so, the peace of God is in your heart. Sorrow and sighing have fled away. You are no longer in doubt of the love of God. You are now experiencing His love. His love is as clear to you as the noonday sun. You can cry aloud, "My song shall be always of the loving kindness of the Lord; with my mouth will I ever be telling of your truth, from one generation to another."

When you believe in this way, you are no longer afraid of hell, death, or the devil who has power of death. You are not painfully afraid of God himself. You have only a tender fear of offending Him.

Do you believe? If so, your soul magnifies the Lord and your spirit rejoices in God, your Savior. You rejoice because you have redemption through Jesus' blood along with the forgiveness of sins. You rejoice in that Spirit of adoption which cries out in your heart, "Abba, Father!" You rejoice in a hope full of immortality. You rejoice in an earnest expectation of all the good things which God has prepared for those who love Him.

Do you now believe? If so, the love of God is now shed abroad in your heart. You love God because He first loved you. Because you now love God, you love your brother, also. Since you are filled with love, peace, and joy, you are also filled with long-suffering, gentleness, fidelity, goodness, meekness, temperance, and all the other fruits of the same Holy Spirit. You have, in a word, whatever dispositions which are holy, heavenly, or divine. Now you can see with the veil taken away. With an open, uncovered face you see the glory of the Lord. You see His glorious love, and the glorious image in which you were created. Now, through faith you are changed into that same image from glory to glory, by the Spirit of the Lord.

This repentance, this faith, this peace, joy, and love is what the world believes to be madness. The wisdom of the world calls this fanaticism, utter distraction. As you change from glory to glory, you as a man of God disregard the worldly critics. Never be moved by any of them. You know in whom you have believed. Let no man steal that treasure. Hold fast to what you have already attained. Hold fast and follow Jesus until you attain all the great and precious promises.

And to you who have not yet known Jesus, do not let vain persons make you ashamed of His gospel. Never be frightened by those who speak evil of the spiritual things about which they know nothing. Seek Him, and God will soon turn your sadness to joy. Get your chin up. In a little while He will take away all of your fears and give you the spirit of soundness. He who saves and justifies is near. It is not He who condemns. It is Christ who died and rose again, who is even now at the right hand of God. He is there making intercession for you now.

Cast yourself on Him, with all your sins, no matter how numerous they are. Do this now, and you will be given entry into the kingdom of our Lord and Savior Jesus Christ.

All those who misunderstand this way to God are in danger of becoming only "almost a Christian" rather than "altogether a Christian."

From "The Way to the Kingdom," *Forty-Four Sermons*, Sermon VII

3

The Almost Christian

Almost thou persuadest me to be a Christian. (Acts 26:28, KJV)

Ever since the Christian religion was in the world, there have been many in every age and nation who were almost persuaded to be Christians. From my own experience, I know that it avails nothing before God to go only this far. Therefore, it is important for us to consider what is implied in being almost a Christian. In addition, we need to know what is implied in being altogether a Christian.

The first thing implied in being almost a Christian is simple heathen honesty. No one should question this. By heathen honesty, I mean that honesty common heathens expect one of another. It is an honesty that many of them usually practice. The rules of honesty teach them they ought not be unjust. They should not take their neighbor's property either by robbery or theft. They are not to oppress the poor nor ever use extortion. They are not to cheat or overreach anyone. In all dealings, they are to defraud no one and are to owe no man anything.

The common heathen also agrees that some attention should be paid to truth as well as justice. As a result, they shun those who lie and call God to witness to the lie. Also disdained is the slanderer of his neighbor and anyone who accuses another falsely. Indeed, they see willful liars as a disgrace to humanity and pests of society.

In addition, there is a degree of love and assistance which they expect from each other. They expect whatever aid anyone can give another, without depriving himself. And this they extend not only in the little things which can be done without any expense or effort, but also to greater needs. This includes feeding the hungry, if they have food to spare, and clothing the naked from their excess. In general, they are expected to give to any that need from the things which they do not need themselves. The first thing implied in being almost a Christian is this basic kind of heathen love.

The second thing implied in being almost a Christian is having a form of godliness. This is the godliness which is prescribed in the gospel of Christ—having the outside of a real Christian. So the almost Christian does nothing which the gospel forbids. He does not take the name of the Lord in vain. He does not curse, but blesses. He does not swear at all. He simply answers with a yes or a no. He keeps the Lord's day holy, and does not allow either his family or guests to profane it. He avoids every word or look which might directly or indirectly lead to violating the gospel. He abstains from all idle conversation. The result is his avoidance of all detraction, backbiting, gossiping, evil speaking, foolish talking, and jesting. He avoids all conversation which is not edifying and which grieves the Holy Spirit.

He abstains from alcohol in excess and from revelings and gluttony. He avoids, as much as he can, all strife and contention. He strives to live continually in peace with everyone. If he is wronged, he does not avenge himself. He never returns evil for evil. He is not a railer, brawler, or scoffer. He does not criticize the faults or infirmities of his neighbor. He does not willingly wrong, hurt, or grieve any man. In all things he speaks and acts by plain rule, whatever you would not have done to you, do not that to another.[1]

In his doing good, the almost Christian does not limit himself to cheap and easy ways of showing kindness. He works and suffers for the good of many. He strives to use all means possible to help those in need of help. In spite of the personal cost and effort, he acts with all his might. He gives this same effort whether it be for his friends or enemies, for an evil or good person. He has no laziness when it comes to doing good to all men, both for their bodies and their souls.

This almost Christian instructs the ignorant, comforts the afflicted, assures the wavering, quickens the good, and reproves the wicked. He works to awaken those who are asleep spiritually. He attempts to lead all those who are seeking God into an understanding of Jesus. His purpose is to get sinners to accept the forgiveness that is in Jesus. His wish is to stir up those who are already saved through faith to lift up the gospel in all things.

So we see that the almost Christian has a form of godliness. He, according to his opportunities, uses all the means of grace as often as possible. He constantly attends church and avoids all improper actions and appearances while there. He is not like some who do not act so properly, even though they have received the saving faith. Many of those who should know and do better act worse than the almost Christian. They come into church gazing around with listlessness or careless indifference. Sometimes they seem to be praying to God, but often are either asleep or reclined in the most convenient posture for sleep. Or, as if they believed God to be asleep, they look around and talk to one another. In this manner, they give no attention to the church service.

But the almost Christian cannot be accused of having only the form and not the content of religion. He is serious about his worship. He pays attention to the services. When he comes for communion, it is not in a careless manner. He attends to communion with an air, gesture, and deportment which speaks nothing else to God but, "God be merciful to me a sinner!"

The almost Christian also sets apart times for daily and family prayer and maintains a seriousness of behavior. In his uniform practice of outward religion, he has the form of godliness.

The almost Christian has one more quality. He has sincerity. By sincerity, I mean a real inward principle of religion. It is from this inward principle that all of his actions come. So, if we do not have this sincere inward religious principle in our life, we do not have even heathen honesty. The sincerity in this person speaks to all the rest of the world. Even the heathen poet says, "The good hate sin through the love of virtue; you, on the contrary, commit no crime that will tell against you through dread of punishment."[2]

Therefore, if a man only avoids doing evil in order to avoid punishment, he has no reward. Such a purpose will not mark even the most harmless man as a "good heathen." The doing of good through the motives of avoiding punishment, the loss of friends, profit, or reputation is inadequate. If from these motives, one abstains from doing evil and does much good while using all the means of grace, he is still just almost a Christian. If there is no better principle in his heart, he is altogether a hypocrite.

Sincerity is necessarily implied in being almost a Christian. There is included a real and hearty desire to serve

God and do His will. It is necessarily implied that he has a sincere wish to please God in all things. He seeks to please God in all his conversations and actions. If a man is almost a Christian, this design runs through all areas of his life. This is the moving principle of his life. It is the cause of his doing good, avoiding evil, and using the ordinances of God.

The next question could well be, "Is it possible that anyone living could go so far as this, and be only almost a Christian? What more must one do or be to become altogether a Christian?"

My answer is that I know from personal experience, and the Word of God, that it is possible to go this far yet be but almost a Christian. I went this far for many years, as I have testified, and was but almost a Christian. I used all diligence to avoid evil and to keep a clear conscience. I was careful of my time, using every opportunity to do good to all men. I was constant and careful in using all means to grace, both public and private. I endeavored to be serious at all times and in all places. With God as my witness, I did this with all sincerity, having a real design to serve Him. It was my full desire to do His will in all things, and to please Him who had called me to fight the good fight to gain eternal life. Now my conscience bears me witness in the Holy Spirit, all that time I was only almost a Christian.

You may now ask, "What more than this is implied in being altogether a Christian?"

The love of God must be in the heart of the altogether Christian. His Word says, "You shall love the Lord your God with all your heart, and with all your soul, and with all your mind."[3] Such a love of God as this engrosses the whole heart. It takes up all of the affections. It fills the capacity of the soul, and employs the fullest extent of all its faculties. Anyone who loves God in this manner is continually rejoicing in God, his Savior. His delight is the Lord—his Lord and his all. In everything he gives thanks to God. All his desire is for God and to the remembrance of His name. His heart is ever crying out, "Whom have I in heaven but you? And there is none upon earth that I desire besides you."

Indeed, what is there to desire besides God? He cannot desire the world or the things of the world. He is crucified to the world, and the world is crucified to him. He is crucified to the desire of the flesh, the desire of the eye, and the pride of life. He dwells in love, dwelling in God, and God in him. He is less than nothing in his own eyes.

The next thing implied in being altogether a Christian is the love of his neighbor. Jesus also commanded his followers to love their neighbor as they loved themselves.[4] It can then be asked, "Who is my neighbor?"

The reply is, every man in the world. Every child of God, the Father of all spirits of all flesh, is your neighbor. In no way may we exclude our enemies or the enemies of God from this requirement. Every Christian must love them just as he loves himself and as Christ loves us.

Paul, in his first letter to the Corinthians describes this love to us. This love is long-suffering and kind. It does not have envy. It is not rash or hasty in loving. It is not proud, or "puffed up." It makes the person with this love the least, the servant of all. Love does not behave itself unbecomingly, but becomes all things to all men. Love seeks not its own way, but only the good of others, that they may be saved. Love is not provoked. It casts out all wrath from him who has been made perfect in love. It thinks no evil, but rejoices in the truth. It covers all things, believes all things, hopes all things, and endures all things.

Still, there is one thing more which is implied in being altogether a Christian. This is the foundation—faith that cannot be separated from love. Faith is spoken of in excellent ways in the Scripture. "Everyone who believes that Jesus is the Christ is a child of God."[5] "But as many as received him, to them gave he power to become the sons of God, even to them that believe on his name."[6] "This is the victory that overcometh the world, even our faith."[7] Our Lord himself declared, "He who believes in the Son has eternal life; he does not come into judgment but has passed from death to life."[8]

Now let no one deceive himself. Carefully note that any faith which does not produce repentance, love, and good works is not a true, living faith. Instead, it is a dead and devilish faith. Even the devils believe that Jesus was born of a virgin. They know that He accomplished all kinds of miracles and declared himself to be God. They also know that, for our sakes, He suffered a most painful death to redeem us from everlasting death. They believe that He rose again on the third day, ascended into heaven, and now sits at the right hand of the Father. They know that He will come at the end of the world to judge both the quick and the dead. Yes, these articles of Christian faith the devils believe, as well as all that is written in the Bible. Yet with all this belief—this faith—they are still devils. They remain in their same damnable condition, lacking the very true Christian saving faith.

The right and true Christian faith is not only to believe the Scriptures and historical doctrines are true. True faith is much more than that. True Christian faith is also to have a sure trust and confidence in God, that by the merits of Jesus, my sins are forgiven, and I am reconciled to God's favor. From this trust and confidence follows a loving heart prone to obey God's commandments.

Whoever has this working faith is altogether Christian. This faith makes it possible to love according to the commandments. It fills the Christian with a love stronger than death, for both God and all mankind. This divine love does the works of God, glorying in being used for all men. It endures with joy any reproach because of Christ. It accepts being mocked, despised, hated, or whatever the wisdom of God permits the malice of men or devils to inflict. Whoever has this faith, thus working by love, is not almost, but altogether a Christian.

Who can agree that these things I have said are true? I ask you to ask yourself about it. With God as your witness, ask your own heart, "Am I altogether a Christian? Do I practice justice, mercy, and truth as the rules of heathen honesty require? Do I have the outside of a Christian? Do I have a form of godliness, abstaining from evil and all that is forbidden in God's Word? Do I do good with all my might? Do I seriously employ all the means of grace and ordinances of God at every opportunity? Do I do all this with a sincere design and desire to please God in all things?"

Most people are aware that they never come even this far. They know they have not been even almost a Christian. Most have not come up to the standard of heathen honesty, at least, nor to the outward form of Christian godliness. Much less has God seen a sincerity, a real desire to please Him in all the things they do.

Few people have ever intended to devote all their words and works, their businesses, studies, and diversions to God's glory. Most have never even desired that what they did would be done in the name of Jesus, the Lord. Few have hoped that their acts would be a spiritual sacrifice acceptable to God through Christ.

However, supposing that there are good desires behind human actions, do these make a Christian? By no means, unless they are brought to good effect. "Hell is paved with good intentions."[9]

The great question still confronts you. Is the love of God shed abroad in your heart? Can you cry out, "My God, and my all"? Do you desire nothing but Him? Are you happy in God? Is He your glory, your delight, your crown of rejoicing? Is this commandment written in your heart, He that loves God loves his brother also? Do you then love your neighbor as yourself? Do you love every man, even your enemies and enemies of God, as your own self? Do you love them as Christ loved you?

Do you believe Christ loved you, and gave himself for you? Do you have faith in the blood sacrifice He made for you? Can you believe the Lamb of God has taken away your sins, and cast them as a stone into the depths of the sea? Do you know He has blotted out any charges that were held against you, taking them away, nailing them to His cross? Have you indeed received this redemption through His blood, including the remission of your sins? Does the Holy Spirit witness to you that you are now a child of God?

The witness of the Word of God is that any man who dies without this faith and love should have never been born. Awake then, you who have been spiritually asleep, and call upon God. Call to Him for faith in the day when He may be found. Let Him not rest until He gives you this goodness. Call to Him until He proclaims to you the name of Jesus. In Him you can know the Lord God, merciful and gracious, long-suffering, and abundant in goodness and truth. He has mercy for all, forgiving iniquity, transgression, and sin.

Let no one convince you, by any words, to stop short of this great prize to which you were called. Call out to Jesus day and night until you know you can believe in Him. Remember that while you were ungodly and without strength, He died so that you might be godly and have strength. So pray always and do not faint until you can lift up your hand to heaven and say, "My Lord and my God!" Then you can declare to Him that lives forever, "Lord, you know all things. You know I love you."

In this manner we all may experience what it is to be, not almost, but altogether Christians. Through His grace, the redemption that is in Jesus, we will be freely justified with this saving faith. We will know we have the peace of God through Jesus Christ. Then we can rejoice in the hope and glory of God and have the love of God shed abroad in our hearts. We will have received all of this faith and love through the Holy Spirit, which will be given unto us.

It is obvious that the grace of God is needed to make us altogether a Christian. Our entire nature must be changed. We must be born anew.

From "The Almost Christian," *Forty-Four Sermons*, Sermon II.

4

The New Birth

You must be born again. (*John 3:7, Phillips*)

If any doctrines within all Christianity may be properly listed as fundamental, they are doubtless these two: the doctrine of justification (salvation), and that of the new birth.

The first relates to the great work that God does *for* us. The second relates to the work that God does *in* us, renewing our fallen nature. In order of time, neither comes before the other. In the same moment we are saved through the grace of God, through the redemption that is in Jesus, we are also born of the Spirit. However, in order of thinking, justification, or salvation, precedes the new birth. We first conceive His wrath being turned away, then His Spirit working in our hearts.

It is of the greatest importance for every person to understand these fundamental doctrines. From a conviction about this importance, many well-qualified writers have dealt extensively with justification, explaining the meaning of the Scriptures which relate to this doctrine. Many others have also written on the new birth. Some of those have written extensively enough, but not as clearly, deeply, and as accurately as required. Too often the result has been either an obscure, obtuse explanation or a slight and superficial one.

There is a need for a clear account of the new birth, a need for a full and satisfactory answer to several basic questions. They are: First, why must we be born again? Or, what is the scriptural foundation of this new birth doctrine? Second, how must we be born again? Or, what is the nature of the new birth? And third, for what purpose must we be born again? Or, to what end is it necessary?

By God's grace, I wish to deal with each of these questions in the following material. Then, I will add a few instances which seem to naturally follow.

First, why must we be born again? What is the foundation or basis of this doctrine?

The foundation of the doctrine of the new birth lies almost as deep as the creation of the world. We may turn to the scriptural account of creation for our first reading. From it we read, "Then God [the triune God] said, 'Let us make man in our image, after our likeness.' So God created man in his own image, in the image of God he created him."[1]

This image of God, in which man was created, includes but is not limited to man's natural image. This natural image includes a spiritual being with understanding, freedom of will, and the various affections. Nor was this image in which man was created limited to the political image. In the political image is included the right to govern the world with dominion over it and its creatures.

The chief image of God in which man was created is His moral image. This, according to Paul, is "true righteousness and holiness."[2] In this image of God, man was made.

"God is love."[3] According to this, at creation man was full

of love in the image of God. Love was the sole principle of all
his emotions, thoughts, words, and actions.

God is full of justice, mercy, and truth. Man was also full of
these qualities as he came from the hands of his creator.

God is purity. In the beginning man was also pure. This
was so because God pronounced him, as well as all the other
works of His creation, as "very good."[4] Man could not have
been pronounced as good had he not been pure from sin, and
filled with righteousness and true holiness. There is no
middle ground. If a person is not loving of God, not righteous
and holy, he is not good. We understand such a person not to
be good at all, much less to be "very good."

Although man was made in the image of God, he was not
made incapable of change. Such limitations would have been
inconsistent with the state in which God was pleased to place
him. He was therefore created able to stand, and yet liable to
fall. God himself warned man of this. Even after this
warning, man did not live in honor and fell from his high
place. Man ate of the tree which God had commanded him to
avoid. By this willful disobedience and rebellion against
God, he openly declared he would govern himself. He
showed that he would not be subject to the will of his creator.
By this act he withdrew from seeking his happiness in God.
Man decided to seek his happiness in the world and the
things of the world.

God had told man before, "In the day that you eat of it [the
tree], you shall die."[5] The Word of the Lord cannot be
broken. Accordingly, on that day, man died. He died to God,
the worst of all deaths. He lost the life of God. He was
separated from Him. This union had been the source of
man's spiritual life. As the body dies when separated from
the soul, the soul dies when separated from God. Man
experienced this separation from God in the very moment he
disobeyed God's command.

There was immediate proof of this spiritual change. Almost immediately the love of God was extinguished in his soul. He was now alienated from the life of God. Instead of love, he was caught up in servile fear. His fear was so great that he fled from the presence of God. Even his remembrance of God was diminished. He was attempting to hide from Him who filled both heaven and earth.[6]

Man had lost both the knowledge and love of God, and without that image, he could not exist as a spiritual creature. Therefore, at the same time, he became both unhappy and unholy. Along with this, he sank into pride and self-will, the very image of the devil. Now in the image of the devil rather than God, he sank into sensual appetites and desires. He matched the image of beasts that perish.

Some may object that the warning, "In the day you eat thereof, you shall surely die," refers only to death of the body. The answer to that objection is plain. Such an occasion would make God a liar, because Adam did not die in that sense. According to the biblical account, Adam lived more than 900 years longer. Therefore, the warning cannot be understood as referring to the death of the body. It must be understood as spiritual death, the loss of life and the image of God.

In Adam all died, all mankind. The children who were to follow him became as their father. The natural consequence is that everyone descended from him comes into the world with the same mind and heart. All are spiritually dead, dead to God, wholly separated from Him in sin. Each man is entirely void of the life of God. All are outside the image of God and His righteousness and holiness, which were originally in Adam.

Instead, each person born into the world now bears the image of the devil in pride and self-will. Each carries the image of a beast through sensual appetites and desires.

This is the foundation and basis of the new birth. Adam's sin resulted in the corruption of our nature. Being born in sin and separated from God, we must be born again. Everyone who is born of a woman must be born again of the Spirit of God. The old nature must be remade into the original godly nature.

Then how must a man be born again? What is the nature of the new birth? This is the second question which deserves more than a slight answer. We need to ponder this in our hearts until we fully understand it. We must clearly see how we are to be born again.

No minute philosophical account of how it is done is available. Jesus warned us against any such expectation in His words which follow His command about the new birth. "The wind blows where it wills [but not by man's power or wisdom], and you hear the sound of it [and are assured beyond all doubt that it does blow], but you do not know whence it comes or whither it goes."[7] How it begins and ends, rises and falls, no man can tell. "So it is with everyone who is born of the Spirit."[8]

You may be assured of the fact of the new birth, just as you are of the blowing of the wind. The precise manner how this is done by the Holy Spirit remains inexplicable. However, it is adequate to explain the nature of the new birth without bothering to explain how it is accomplished by God. This will satisfy most men who are in search of a salvation experience through the new birth.

The expression, "being born again," was not first used by Jesus in the recorded conversation with Nicodemus. It was well known before that time. It was in common use among the Jews when Jesus was born. When an adult heathen was converted to the Jewish religion, it was the custom to baptize and circumcise him. When he was baptized, he was said to be born again. This expression meant that he who had been a child of the devil was now adopted into the family of God. He was now considered one of God's children.

In the case at hand, Jesus was using the expression in a stronger sense than the earlier Jewish context. Nicodemus ought to have understood the original meaning. He may well have recognized Jesus' new meaning when he asked his next question, "How can this be?"[9]

Literally, a man cannot enter a second time into his mother's womb to be born again. But all men may be born again from above. Each may be born of the Spirit, born of God in a manner which bears a close analogy to the natural birth.

Before a child is born into the world he has eyes, but cannot see. He has ears, but cannot hear. He has an imperfect use of the other senses. He has no knowledge of any of the things of the world, or any natural understanding. To that early manner of existence, we do not give the name "life." It is only when a man is born that we say he begins to live.

When the child is born, he begins to breathe and live in a wholly different manner from what he did before. He begins to see light. Only then can he begin to perceive the objects around him. His ears are then opened, and he hears the sounds which strike his eardrums. At the same time, all the other organs of sense begin to be exercised upon their proper objects.

This parallel holds true in both the natural birth and the spiritual birth. While a man is in a mere natural state, before he is born of God, he has, in a spiritual sense, eyes and does not see. A thick impenetrable veil lies upon them. He has ears, but he does not hear. He is utterly deaf to what he needs most of all to hear. His other spiritual senses are all locked up. He is in the same condition as if he did not even have them.

The result is that he has no knowledge of God. He has no relationship with Him. He is not even acquainted with Him. He has no true knowledge of the things of God, either spiritual or eternal. Therefore, though he is a living man, he is a dead Christian. But as soon as he is born of God, there is a total change in all these particulars. The eyes of his understanding are opened, according to Paul.[10] God commands the light which shines out of darkness to shine upon the heart.

The man then sees the light of the glory of God. He sees His glorious love in the face of Jesus Christ.

His ears are now opened and are capable of hearing the inward voice of God. This voice says, "Take heart, my son; your sins are forgiven."[11] "Go, and sin no more."[12] This is the content of what God speaks to his heart, although perhaps not in these exact words. He is now ready to hear whatever the Holy Spirit is pleased to reveal to him.

He feels in his heart the mighty working of the Spirit of God. This feeling is not in the carnal sense, as the men of the world mistakenly understand the expression, although they have been told again and again its meaning. The meaning is only this, he feels or is inwardly aware of the graces which the Spirit of God works in his heart. He feels and is conscious of a peace which passes all understanding. He many times feels a joy in God that is unspeakable and full of glory. He feels the love of God shed abroad in his heart by the Holy Spirit which has been given to him. All of his spiritual senses are used to discern spiritual good and evil. He is increasing daily in his knowledge of God and understanding about the inward kingdom of heaven.

Now he may be properly said to live. God has awakened his spirit. He is alive to God through Jesus Christ. He lives a life the world cannot know outside such a relationship. His is a life hidden with Christ in God.

God continually breathes, in a manner of speaking, upon his soul. His soul is continually breathing to God. Grace is descending into his heart. His prayer and praise ascends to heaven. By this conversation between God and man, a kind of spiritual respiration is set up. Through this, the life of God in the soul is sustained, and this fellowship with the Father and the Son grows. In this manner, the child of God grows up, until he comes to full measure of stature in Christ.

It clearly appears what the new birth is. Its nature is that great change which God works in the soul when He brings it to life. The new birth is how He raises the soul from death in sin to the life of righteousness. It is the change wrought in the whole soul by the almighty Spirit of God when the soul is created anew in Christ Jesus and renewed after the image of God in righteousness and true holiness. It is when the love of the world is changed into the love of God. Pride is then changed into humility, and passion into meekness. Hatred, envy, and malice are replaced by sincere, tender, unselfish love for all mankind. In a word, it is that change whereby the earthly, sensual, devilish mind is turned into the mind which was in Christ Jesus. That is the nature of the new birth. It is the nature of everyone who is born of the Holy Spirit.

It is not difficult for any who have thought about these things to see the necessity of the new birth. From these considerations comes the answer to the third question. To what end is it necessary that we should be born again?

It is easily discerned that the new birth is necessary to gain holiness. What is holiness? What is it according to the Scriptures? It is not a bare external religion, a list of outward duties. No matter how many duties be performed or how exactly they are performed, they are not holiness.

Gospel holiness is nothing less than the image of God stamped upon the heart. Holiness is nothing other than the whole mind which was in Jesus. It consists of all heavenly affections and tempers mingled together into one attitude. Holiness implies a continual, thankful love to Him who has not withheld His Son from us. This gift of His only Son makes it natural and necessary for us to love every person in the world. It fills us with a heart of mercy, kindness, gentleness, and long-suffering. It is a love of God that teaches us to be faultless in all conversation. It enables us to present our souls and bodies—all we have and all we are—as a continual sacrifice to God. All our thoughts, words, and actions are to be acceptable to Christ Jesus.

Obviously, this holiness can have no existence in us until the image of our mind is renewed. It cannot begin in the soul until that change is wrought. This cannot occur until the power of God overshadows us and we are brought from darkness to light. Then we are taken from the power of Satan and placed under the power of God. All this occurs when we are born again, which is absolutely necessary to regain original holiness.

Without holiness no man shall see the Lord, and see the face of God in glory. Consequently, the new birth is absolutely necessary to receive eternal salvation.

Men may flatter themselves that they may live in their sins until their last breath, and still have eternal life with God. Thousands believe this. They really believe they have found a broad way of life which does not lead to eternal destruction.

Looking around, they say, "What danger is there to a person who is harmless and virtuous? What fear is there to an honest man? Can one of strict morality miss heaven? And what about those who continually attend church and accept its sacraments?"

"Surely I will do as well as my neighbors," another affirms with all assurance.

Yes, as well as the unholy neighbor. Such a man will die in

his sins. All will drop into the pit together. Then and there, in due time, you will see the necessity of holiness to see the glory of God.

Consequently, this is the necessity of the new birth. Since none can be holy unless he is born again, none can see God except he is born again. Without holiness, no man shall see the Lord.

For this same reason, no man can be happy in this world unless he is born again. It is not possible, in the nature of things, that a man should be happy who is not holy. Even the poor ungodly poet Juvenal tells us, *Nemo malus felix* ("no wicked man is happy"). The reason is plain. All unholy emotions are unhappy emotions. Malice, hatred, envy, jealousy, and revenge create a present hell in the heart. Even easier passions, if not kept under control, give a thousand times more pain than pleasure. Even hope, when stalled, makes the heart sick. Every desire which is not according to the will of God is liable to pierce us through with many sorrows.

All the general sources of sin—pride, self-will, and idolatry—are in the same proportion sources of misery. Therefore, as long as they reign in any soul, happiness cannot exist there. But they must reign until our basic nature is changed, that is, until we are born again. Consequently, the new birth is absolutely necessary to have happiness in this world, as well as in the world to come.

I proposed in the last place to state a few inferences, which naturally follow from the preceding observations.

The first of these is that baptism is not the new birth. Baptism and the new birth are not one and the same thing. Many seem to imagine they are the same. At least, they speak as if they think so. Such an opinion is not publicly accepted by any denomination of Christians. Certainly it is not by any that I know.

The judgment of my church is clear. It is stated in church teaching that there are two parts to any sacrament. One is the outward and visible sign, and the other is the inward spiritual grace signified by the outward sign.

In regard to baptism, it is a sacrament ordained by Christ. The outward sign is the washing with water, signifying the seal of regeneration (rebirth) by His Spirit. So it is absolutely clear that baptism is separate from the thing signified. The outward sign is distinct from the inward regeneration.

The catechism states the meaning of the word sacrament with utmost clearness. A sacrament is an outward and visible sign of an inward and spiritual grace. The outward form of the sacrament of baptism is water, wherein a person is baptized in the name of the Father, Son, and Holy Spirit. The inward part of the thing is death to sin and a new birth to righteousness. Nothing is plainer, according to this, that baptism is not the new birth.

However, the rationale of the matter is so clear and evident that we need no other authority than that reasonable evidence. What can be more plain than that one is external and the other is internal. One is a visible work, and the other is an invisible work. Therefore, each is wholly different from the other. One is an act of man purifying the body. The other is a change wrought by God in the soul, purifying it. By this, the former is just as distinguishable from the latter as is the soul from the body. Certainly water is distinguishable from the Holy Spirit.

From these reflections, we may next observe that as the new birth is not the same as baptism, so it does not always accompany baptism. These two do not always go together. A person may be baptized with water and yet not be born of the Spirit. There may sometimes be the outward sign where there is not the inward grace. I do not now speak with regard to infants. It is certain that the historical church supposes that all who are baptized in their infancy are at the same time born again.

But whatever may be the case for infants, it is sure that those of more maturity are not necessarily born again at baptism. The tree is known by its fruits. From this, it is too plain to be denied that many who belonged to the devil before baptism continue to belong to him after it. The works of their father they continue to do. They continue to be servants of Satan in sin, without any pretense toward either inward or outward holiness.

A third inference which we may draw from what has been observed is that the new birth is not the same as sanctification. Many have taken it for granted that both are the same. Thus they believe that the new birth —regeneration—is a progressive work carried out in the soul by slow degrees, from our first turning to God. This is true of sanctification, but is not true of the new birth. The new birth is a part of sanctification—being made perfect in the image of God. However, the new birth is not the whole of sanctification. It is the gate into it. When we are born again, our sanctification—our inward and outward holiness—begins. From then on, we gradually grow up in Jesus who is our Lord.

The expression used by Paul, to "grow up in every way into him who is the head," illustrates the difference between the two.[13] It points out the exact analogy between natural and spiritual things. A child is born of a woman in a moment, or at least in a very short time. Afterwards, he gradually and slowly grows until he attains the stature of a man. In like manner, a child is born of God in a short time, if not in a moment. But it is by slow degrees that he later grows up to the measure of the full stature of Christ. The same relationship which is between our natural birth and growth is also between our new birth and our final perfection.

Another point which we may learn from the preceding concerns our obligation to others. This is a point of great importance which deserves lengthy consideration. What can the reborn person who loves all mankind say to those who are still in sin and unregenerated? He must say to them, "You must be born again."

The sinner himself may say, "I defy your doctrine. I do not need to be born again. I was born again when I was baptized. Are you telling me to deny my baptism?"

The answer is simple. First, there is nothing in the world which will excuse a lie. Therefore we must say to the baptized sinner, "If you have been baptized, do not admit it. Such an admission really aggravates your guilt. You claim that you were devoted and dedicated to God at your baptism. Now, all these years since then you have been devoted to the devil. Look at the way you live.

"Before you were old enough to have reason, you were consecrated to God the Father, the Son, and the Holy Spirit. Since then, after the age of reason, you have been flying in the face of God, consecrating yourself to Satan by doing his works. Does love of the world, pride, anger, lust, foolish desire, and a whole train of such affections stand in your life where they should not? Are you allowing all of these miserable emotions to live in a soul which was once a temple of the Holy Spirit? If you were baptized, your soul had been set apart for an habitation of God through the Spirit. It had been solemnly given up to Him. And you now glory in this, that you once belonged to God? It is time to be ashamed. You should never boast of what you are denying before God and man."

Any life of sin denies the baptism in the most effectual manner. Sinners deny their baptism thousands of times. They still do it every day. In your baptism you renounce the devil and his works. Therefore, whenever you allow Satan a place in your life and do any works of the devil, you deny your baptism. So, you deny it by every willful sin. You deny it by every act of uncleanness, drunkenness, or revenge. You deny it by every obscene or profane word, by every oath that comes out of your mouth. Every time you profane the day of the Lord, you deny your baptism. You deny God and your baptism every time you do anything to another which you would not have them do to you.

Whether you are baptized or not, you must be born again. Otherwise, it is not possible for you to be inwardly holy. Without inward as well as outward holiness, you cannot be happy in either this world or the world to come.

Perhaps you say, "But I do no harm to anyone. I am honest and just in my dealings. I do not curse or take the Lord's name in vain. I do not profane the Lord's day. I am not a drunkard. I do not slander my neighbor or live in any willful sin."

If this were true, it would be well if all men were as good as you. But, you must go further still, or you cannot be saved.

Do you claim that you do go further? "I go further yet, for I not only do no harm, but do all the good I can."

I really doubt that. There are thousands of opportunities for doing good which are allowed to pass without action, for which there is an account to be made to God. But even if you have done good in all of these situations, done all you possibly could to all men, you still must be born again. Without the new birth, nothing will help your poor, sinful, polluted soul.

But you object, "I constantly attend to all the ordinances of God. I go to my church and do all that it requires."

It is good that you do that. But this will not keep you out of sin and hell. That can be accomplished only by being born again. Go to church twice a day. Go to the Lord's table every week. Say innumerable prayers in private. Hear many good sermons. Read many good books. Still, you must be born again. No outward practices will stand in the place of the new birth. Nothing under heaven will stand in its place.

If you have not already experienced this inward work of God, the new birth, add one thing more. Pray continually, "Lord, add this to all my blessings, let me be born again. Deny me whatever you please, but let me be born again. Take away from me whatever is necessary, only give me this. Take away my reputation, fortune, friends, and health, but let me be born again of the Holy Spirit. Let me be received among the children of God. Let me be born incorruptible by the Word of God, which lives and abides forever." Then, after the new birth, pray, "Let me daily grow in grace, and in the knowledge of our Lord and Savior Jesus Christ."

When this is done, the new birth will be given. The Holy Spirit comes into the soul and gives a witness of His presence. We receive inward assurance of His work and indwelling presence.

From "The New Birth," *Forty-Four Sermons*, Sermon XXXIX.

5

Marks of the New Birth

So it is with every one who is born of the Spirit. (John 3:8)

How is everyone who is born of the Holy Spirit, who is born again, born of God? What is meant by being born again, being born of God, or being born of the Holy Spirit? What is implied in being a son or a child of God, of having the Spirit of adoption? We know these privileges are ordinarily related to baptism, which is termed by Jesus in the preceding verse: being born of water and of the Spirit. Now we want to know what these privileges are.

Perhaps it is not necessary to give a definition of this because the Scripture gives none. But the question is important to all people. Unless a man is born again, born of the Holy Spirit, he cannot enter into the kingdom of God. Here are the marks of the new birth as I find them in Scripture.

The first mark is faith. It is the foundation of all of the rest. Thus Paul said, "Ye are all the children of God by faith in Christ Jesus."[1] And John said, "To them gave he power to become the sons of God, even to them that believe on his name, which were born not of blood, nor of the will of the flesh, nor of the will of man, but of God."[2] And again in his general epistle John wrote, "Whosoever believeth that Jesus is the Christ is born of God."[3]

These apostles were not writing about a speculative faith. This faith is not the bare assent to the proposition, Jesus is the Lord. It is not mere agreement with all the propositions contained in the creeds, or in the whole Bible. It is not merely an agreement to any or all those believable things as believable. Devils have this much belief. To say that this belief is faith would be to say that devils are born of God. They believe both that Jesus is the Christ, and that all Scripture is true, having been given by inspiration from God. Theirs is not only a belief in divine truth, the testimony of God, or the evidence of miracles. Those spirits heard the words from Jesus' mouth and knew He was a faithful and true witness. They could not help receiving the testimony He gave, both of himself, and of God, who sent Him. They also saw the mighty works He did and believed that He came forth from God. Regardless of this much faith and belief, they are still devils who await the judgment of hell on the last day.

Such belief is no more than a dead faith. The true, living Christian faith is that which works in those who are born of God. The necessary faith is not only an assent through understanding, but a disposition which God brings about to give the believer a confidence in God. It is a conviction arising from that confidence that our sins are forgiven through the merits of Jesus. We know that we are now reconciled to God.

This implies first that a man must renounce himself. To be found in Christ, to be accepted through Him, he must totally reject all confidence he has in himself and his own works. He has nothing to pay, and has no trust in his own works or righteousness of any kind. He comes to God as a lost, miserable, self-destroyed, self-condemned, undone, and helpless sinner. At last his mouth is utterly closed. He knows he is altogether guilty before God.

Such a sense of sin is commonly called despair by those who criticize the faith they do not understand. This sense of sin must be coupled with a full conviction that no words can express. It is the conviction that our salvation comes only through Jesus.

There is also an awareness that a real desire for salvation must precede a living, trusting faith in Jesus. His life and His death were the fulfillment of the law for all of us. Faith then, by which we are born of God, is not simply a belief in all of the articles of our faith. It is more than that. It is a true confidence in the mercy of God through our Lord Jesus Christ.

There is an immediate and constant fruit of this faith, whereby we are born of God. It is a fruit that cannot be separated from it at any time. This fruit is power over sin. It is power over outward sin of every kind. It is power over every evil word and work. It is power through the blood of Christ when applied. This power purges the conscience from dead works and from inward sin. The power over inward sin purifies the heart from every unholy desire and temper.

Paul describes this fruit of faith in the sixth chapter of his letter to the Romans. There he wrote, "How can we who died to sin still live in it?"[4] Our old personality is crucified with Christ, so that the body of the sin in us might be destroyed. Now we no longer have to serve sin. We are now dead to sin, but alive to God through Jesus Christ our Lord. Sin no longer reigns in the mortal body. We yield ourselves to God as those who are now alive from the dead. Sin has no dominion over us, thanks be to God. Once we were servants of sin, but now we have been made free through the work of

Jesus. Plainly, we simply thank God. We were in the past servants of sin. Now we are free from sin and have become servants of righteousness.

This same priceless privilege of the sons of God was also confirmed by the Apostle John. He was particularly sure of the power over outward sin. He wrote, "Behold, what manner of love the Father hath bestowed upon us, that we should be called the sons of God. . . . Beloved, now are we the sons of God, and it doth not yet appear what we shall be, but we know that, when he shall appear, we shall be like him; for we shall see him as he is."[5] Then John wrote, "Whosoever is born of God doth not commit sin; for his seed remaineth in him, and he cannot sin, because he is born of God."[6]

Being unable to understand this, some men will say, "True, whoever is born of God does not commit sin, habitually." The conditioning of the Scripture with the word "habitually" would allow occasional sin. This is a deception which alters God's promise given by John. Adding this condition brings the promise of God to no effect. Beware that you do not add the word "habitually" to condition this Scripture in your mind, if not in your words.

John interprets his own words: "You know that he appeared to take away sins, and in him there is no sin."[7] From this comes the inference in the following verse: "No one who abides in him sins; no one who sins has either seen him or known him."[8] John knew that men would try to persuade Christians that they could commit sin and still be the children of God. He cautions us: "Little children, let no one deceive you. He who does right is righteous, as he is righteous. He who commits sin is of the devil; for the devil has sinned from the beginning. . . . No one born of God commits sin, for God's nature abides in him, and he cannot sin, because he is born of God. By this it may be seen who are the children of God, and who are the children of the devil."[9]

By this plain mark of committing or not committing sins, men are distinguished one from the other. The same meaning is in the fifth chapter. "We know that anyone born of God does not sin, but he who was born of God keeps him, and the evil one does not touch him."[10]

Another fruit of the living faith is peace. In being saved by faith, we have all our sins blotted out. "We have peace with God through our Lord Jesus Christ."[11] This is what Jesus himself promised all His followers the night before His death. He said, "Peace I leave with you; my peace I give to you; not as the world gives do I give to you. Let not your hearts be troubled, neither let them be afraid."[12] And again He said, "These things I have spoken unto you, that in me ye might have peace."[13]

This is that peace of God which passes all understanding. It is a peace which is impossible for even the spiritual man to describe. It is a peace which all of the powers of the earth and hell are unable to shake. Waves and storms can beat upon it but they cannot shake it, for it is founded upon a rock. It keeps the hearts and minds of the children of God at all times and in all places. Whether they are in comfort or in pain, in sickness or health, in abundance or need, they are happy in God. In every state they have learned to be content and to give thanks to God through Jesus Christ. They are completely assured that whatever is best for them will happen to them. The result is that through all the hardships of life, they stand fast in peace, believing in the Lord.

Another scriptural mark of those who are born of God is hope. Peter wrote about this. He said, "Blessed be the God and Father of our Lord Jesus Christ! By his great mercy we have been born anew to a living hope."[14] Peter described this hope as a living hope, because there is a dead hope just as there is a dead faith. There is a hope which is not from God, but from Satan. Dead hope is evidenced by its fruits.

Dead hope is the offspring of pride and is the parent of every evil word and work. Everyone with living hope is holy, as God who called him to be holy. Every man who can truly say, "Beloved, now are we the sons of God . . . for we shall see him as he is," has a living hope. He believes that he can be purified even as God himself is pure. This is his hope.

This hope implies the testimony of our own spirit or conscience, that we walk in simplicity and godly sincerity. It also implies that we receive the testimony of the Spirit of God bearing witness to our spirit that we are His children. In knowing that we are His children, we know that we are heirs of God and fellow heirs with Christ.

God himself teaches us about this great privilege of His children. Who is it that is said to bear the witness? Not our spirit only, but the Spirit of God. God himself is He who bears witness to our spirit. What is it to which He gives witness? That we are His children. "That we are children of God, and if children, then heirs, heirs of God and fellow heirs with Christ." It is in all of the children of God that the Spirit of God bears this witness. So Paul can say in the preceding verses, "For all who are led by the Spirit of God are sons of God." Additionally, he expresses this hope as, "For you did not receive the spirit of slavery to fall back into fear, but you have received the spirit of sonship. When we cry, 'Abba, Father!' it is the Spirit himself bearing witness with our spirit that we are the children of God."[15]

You have received the spirit of adoption whereby you can cry, "Abba, Father!" Who is it that received this spirit of adoption? You, as many as are the sons of God, have, in virtue of your sonship, received that spirit of adoption. Now you can cry out, "Abba, Father." You are now ministers of Christ and stewards of the mysteries of God. You have one Lord, so you have one Spirit. You have one faith, so you have one hope, also. You are sealed with one spirit of promise. The proof of your inheritance is that same Holy Spirit bearing witness with your own spirit that you are the children of God.

Through this, the great beatitude is fulfilled: "Blessed are those who mourn, for they shall be comforted."[16] It is easy to see that some sorrow may precede this witness of God's Spirit with our spirit. In fact, some sorrow must precede it, because we suffer from fear while in separation from God. In that separation we have a sense of the judgment of God abiding on us. As soon as this fruit of hope, through the gift of the Holy Spirit comes upon us, our sorrow and fear is turned to joy. Anguish is no more, because joy belongs to those born of God. It may be many of you now have sorrow because you are aliens from this great promise. Sorrow comes from an awareness within ourselves that we do not have the Holy Spirit. Sorrow is the fruit of those who are without hope and without God in this world. It is only when the Holy Spirit comes that your heart can rejoice. Then your joy will be full.[17] Then you will understand and be able to say, "We join God through our Lord Jesus Christ, by whom we have now received the atonement." We will be able to agree with Paul on this state of grace, of reconciliation with God, "By whom also we have access by faith into this grace wherein we stand, and rejoice in hope of the glory of God."[18]

You have been born again to a lively hope and are kept there by the power of God. You can greatly rejoice in your salvation, even though there may be heaviness through many temptations in this world. There is always praise, honor, and glory to the Lord Jesus Christ even in hours of trial. Through the rebirth and its hope we rejoice with inexpressible joy, being filled with the glory of Jesus Christ even though we do not see him.[19]

How unspeakable His glory is! Man cannot find words to

describe this joy in the Holy Spirit. It is the hidden bread of life which no man can know until he receives it from God. But this we do know, this joy remains in all things and overflows in the very depths of afflictions. Large consolations come from God for His children after all earthly comforts fail. When sufferings most abound, the consolation of His Holy Spirit abounds even more. With this grace, the sons of God can laugh at destruction when it comes. In need, pain, hell, and the grave, they know He has overcome. He has the keys to death and hell. He has ended both for His children. Now the great Holy Spirit comes as though out of heaven saying, "Behold, the tabernacle of God is with men, and he will dwell with them, and they shall be his people, and God himself shall be with them, and be their God. And God shall wipe away all tears from their eyes; and there shall be no more death, neither sorrow, nor crying, neither shall there be any more pain, for the former things are passed away."[20]

Love is the next scriptural mark of those who are born of God. It is the greatest of all the marks of the new birth. "God's love has been poured into our hearts through the Holy Spirit which has been given to us."[21] This is because we are sons of God and God has sent forth His Holy Spirit into our hearts so that we can now cry out, "Abba, Father!"[22] By the Holy Spirit, we continually look to God as our forgiving and loving Father. We call to Him for our daily bread, for all things needed, for both our souls or bodies. We continually pour out our hearts before Him, knowing that He hears our petitions and will give us our requests.[23]

Our delight is in Him. He is the joy of our heart. He is our shield and our exceeding great reward. The desire of our soul is for God. Our whole purpose is to do His will. We are satisfied with whatever He gives, and we speak our praises to Him.

In this same sense we not only love God but we love His

Son, Jesus Christ.[24] We rejoice in our Savior. We love the Lord Jesus Christ with sincerity. We are also joined to the Lord in one spirit, the Holy Spirit. Our soul hangs upon Jesus and chooses Him as altogether lovely. We know and feel what it means, "My beloved is mine and I am his."[25] Our song is now, "You are the fairest of the sons of men; grace is poured upon your lips; therefore, God has blessed you forever."[26]

Love of our neighbor necessarily flows out of our love of God. We love every soul that God has made, even our enemies. Now we can love every man as we love ourselves, as we love our own souls. Jesus commanded this, teaching us to love one another even as He loves us. The result is that this commandment is written on the hearts of all of those who love God. Now we understand this to be the love of God which He expressed for us. He laid down His life that we might be saved. We must then be willing to lay down our lives for our brethren. When we know that we are ready to do this, we truly love our neighbor. By this mark, we know that we have passed from death into life.[27] By this we know that we are born of God and that we dwell in Him, and He in us. We know this because He has given us His loving Spirit. Love is of God. Everyone who loves in this manner is born of God and knows God.[28]

The Apostle John also says, "This is the love of God, that we keep his commandments."[29] His commandment is that we love our neighbor in the same way that we love God. This is the sign or proof of the love of God. It is the keeping of the first and great commandment. True love, once poured into our hearts, will cause us to do so. Whoever loves God with all of his heart will serve Him with all of his strength in all of His commandments.

Universal obedience to Him whom we love is another fruit

of the love of God. It is a desire to conform to His will. It is an obedience to all of His commands, both external and internal. It is an obedience of the heart and of the entire life. It is an obedience in love through our every emotion and in all our conversation. One of the most obvious implications of this is being zealous of all good works. There is always a hungering and thirsting to do good in every possible way to all men. There is a rejoicing in being given and being able to give for all men. There is no seeking of any reward in this world for this service and obedience. The child of God only seeks resurrection to eternal life for the forgiven and justified.

These are the marks of the new birth which are laid down in the Scripture. God himself answers the question, "What is it to be born of God?" Everyone who is born of the Holy Spirit believes in God through Christ. The child of God does not commit sin. At all times and in all places he enjoys the peace of God which passes all understanding. He has the testimony of his own conscience and of the Holy Spirit that he is a child of God. From this springs continual rejoicing in his forgiveness and acceptance. The result is a love for God which far exceeds any love ever known for anyone or anything. This love of God requires that he love all men just as he loves himself. This love is not hidden in the heart alone, but flames out in all action and conversation.

The reborn Christian's whole life becomes a labor of love in continual obedience to God's commands. Thus the child of God seeks to be merciful even as God is merciful. He yearns for holiness, as God is holy. He seriously seeks to be as perfect as God is perfect.

Each man knows what God has given him. Those who are children of God know it from the trust that is in their hearts. Everyone who has thought about these things knows at this very moment if he is a child of God. Assurance is necessary now. The question is not "were you ever a child of God?" Our conscience asks us about now. What are we now? Is the Holy Spirit now in the heart with assurance?

It is to one's own heart that the appeal must be made. The heart and conscience ask whether you are now the temple of the Holy Spirit. Does the Holy Spirit now dwell in you? Does the Spirit of Jesus and of glory now rest upon you? Or, are you now dead in trespasses and sins?

The born-again child of God is free from self-justification. He has received the next great fruit of the Spirit, release from guilt and condemnation.

From "The Marks of the New Birth," *Forty-Four Sermons*, Sermon XIV.

6

First Fruit of the Holy Spirit

There is therefore now no condemnation to them which are in Christ Jesus, who walk not after the flesh, but after the Spirit. (Romans 8:1, KJV)

Those who are in Christ Jesus are those who truly believe in Him, according to St. Paul. They are those who being justified, pardoned, and saved by faith experience peace with God through our Lord Jesus Christ. They who thus believe no longer walk after the flesh. They no longer follow the inclinations of sinful nature. They now follow after the Holy Spirit. All their thoughts, words, and works are under the blessed Spirit of God.

There is therefore no condemnation to them from God. He has justified them freely by His grace through the redemption that is in Jesus. He has forgiven all their iniquities. He has erased all of their sin. And there is no condemnation to them from within themselves. They have received not the spirit of the world, but the Holy Spirit which is from God. Now they may know the things that are freely given to them from God.[1] The Holy Spirit bears witness with their spirits that they are children of God. To this is added the testimony of their conscience, that in simplicity and godly sincerity, not with human wisdom, but by the grace of God, they have had their conversation (relationship) with the world.[2]

This Scripture has been frequently misunderstood in dangerous ways. Multitudes of men, untaught by God, have consequently altered the truth which leads to godliness and misused it to their own destruction. Therefore, I propose to show, as clearly as I can, several things. First, those who are in Christ Jesus, who walk not after the flesh, but after the Spirit. Second, how there is no condemnation to them. Then, I shall add some practical conclusions.

Who are those who are in Christ Jesus? They are those who believe in His name, who are found in Him, not having their own righteousness, but the righteousness which is of God by faith. They who have redemption through His blood are properly said to be in Him. They dwell in Christ, and Christ dwells in them. They are joined to the Lord in one Spirit. They are ingrafted into Him as branches into the vine. They are united as branches to their head, in a manner which words cannot express. Never before could their hearts have conceived such a union.

Now whoever lives in Him does not sin. He does not walk after the flesh. The flesh, in the usual language of Paul, signifies corrupt human nature. In this sense he uses the words, in writing to the Galatians, "the works of the flesh are plain."[3] A little before he wrote, "Walk by the Spirit, and do not gratify the desires of the flesh." This proves that those who walk by the Spirit do not fulfill the lusts of the flesh. Paul immediately added, "for the desires of the flesh are against the Spirit, and the desires of the Spirit are against the flesh; for these are opposed to each other, to prevent you from doing what you would."[4]

So the words are not to be literally translated, "so that you cannot do the things which you would." It is not as if the flesh overcame the Spirit. Such a translation not only has nothing to do with the original text, but it makes the whole argument worth nothing. It asserts the reverse of what Paul is proving.

They who are of Christ, who abide in Him, have crucified the flesh with its affections and lusts. They abstain from all of those works of the old nature. They abstain from adultery, fornication, uncleanness, lasciviousness, idolatry, witchcraft, hatred, variance, emulations, wrath, strife, sedition, heresy, envy, murders, drunkenness, and revellings. They avoid every design, word, and work to which the corruption of human nature leads. Although they feel the root of bitterness in themselves, they are yet endued with power from God to keep it underfoot continually. It cannot spring up to trouble them. Every fresh assault from the flesh which they experience only gives them fresh occasion to praise God. They continually cry out, "Thanks be to God who gives us the victory through Jesus Christ our Lord."

They now walk after the Spirit, both in their hearts and in their lives. They are taught by the Holy Spirit to love God and their neighbor with a love which is springing up to everlasting life. By the Holy Spirit, they are led into every holy desire. They are led into every divine and heavenly temper, until every thought which arises in their heart is holiness to God.

They who walk after the Holy Spirit are led by Him into all holiness of conversation. Their speech is always in grace, seasoned with salt. It is a conversation based upon the love and fear of God. No corrupt conversation comes out of their mouth. They speak only that which is good, that which is to the use of edifying. They seek always to minister grace to their hearers. So they engage themselves, day and night, in doing only those things which please God. In all their outward behavior, they seek to follow Jesus who left us an example that we might walk in His steps. In all their relations with their neighbors, they attempt to walk in justice, mercy, and truth. Whatever they do, in every circumstance, they do it all to the glory of God.

Being filled with faith and the Holy Spirit, Christians possess in their hearts and show forth in their lives the genuine fruits of the Spirit of God. In their words and actions, they express love, joy, peace, long-suffering, gentleness, goodness, fidelity, meekness, and temperance. They reflect whatever is lovely and praiseworthy. They adorn in all things the gospel of God, our Savior. They give full proof to all mankind that they are indeed moved by the same Holy Spirit which raised Jesus from the dead.

There is no condemnation to them who are thus in Christ Jesus, and walk not after the flesh, but after the Spirit. To these believers in Christ, walking in this way, there is no condemnation because of their past sins. God does not condemn them. It is as though their sins were cast as a stone into the depths of the sea. God does not even remember them. Having set forth Jesus to be the reconciling sacrifice for them, through faith in His blood atonement, God has forgiven them. He has declared to them, Jesus' righteousness is for the remission of all sins that are past. Therefore, none of these past sins are charged to the saved Christian. The memory of them has perished with them.

Now there is no condemnation in their own heart. They have no sense of guilt or dread of the wrath of God. They have the witness in themselves that they are cleansed by the blood of the atonement. They have not received again the spirit of fear. They are not in bondage to wracking doubt and uncertainty. They have received the Spirit of adoption.

They cry out in their heart, "Abba, Father." Having been justified by their faith, they have the peace of God ruling in their hearts. This peace flows from a continuing sense of His pardoning mercy. It is the answer of a good conscience toward God.

It is true that sometimes a believer in Christ may lose this sight of God's mercy. Sometimes darkness may fall upon him so that he no longer sees his God who is invisible. He can come to a point where he no longer feels the witness in himself of his part of the atoning blood. Then, he is inwardly condemned. He has taken on the sentence of death in himself.

When this occurs, he is no longer a believer. He does not see and experience the mercy of God, and has lost faith. Faith implies light. It implies the light of God shining upon the soul. Therefore, if anyone loses this light, he for the time loses his faith. And there is no doubt that a true believer in Christ may lose this light of faith. When that is lost, he may for a time fall into condemnation.

So long as he believes, and walks after the Spirit, a man is not condemned, either by God or his own heart. He is not condemned for any present sins, because he is not now transgressing the commands of God. Not walking after the flesh, but after the Spirit, is continual proof of his love of God. John bears witness to this, "No one born of God commits sin; for God's nature abides in him, and he cannot sin because he is born of God."[5] He cannot commit sin as long as that nature of God, that loving Holy Spirit, abides in him. So long as he keeps himself in the faith, Satan cannot touch or lead him. Now it is evident he is not condemned for sins which he does not commit. They, therefore, who are thus led by the Spirit, are not under the law or under its curse of condemnation.[6] The law condemns only those who break it. Thus the law of God, "Thou shall not steal," convicts none but those who steal. Thus, "Remember the sabbath day and keep it holy," condemns only those who do not keep it holy. Against the fruits of the Spirit, there is no law. Paul more completely explains this in his letter to Timothy. "We know that the law is good, if anyone uses it lawfully, understanding this, that the law is not laid down for the just, but for the lawless and disobedient, for the ungodly and sinners, for the unholy and profane, in accordance with the glorious gospel of the blessed God."[7]

While inward sin does remain, it cannot condemn the believer. The corruption of man's nature still remains, even in those who are the children of God by faith. God's children can still have in them the seeds of pride, anger, vanity, lust, and evil desire. Our daily experience makes it plain that the seeds of every kind of sin can remain in Christians.

Paul, speaking to those he has just affirmed to be in Jesus Christ, still says, "I, brethren, could not address you as spiritual men, but as men of the flesh, as babes in Christ."[8] From this we see that they were babes in Christ. They were in Christ, but they were believers in a low degree. From this we see that sin remained in them. They had a fleshly mind which was not subject to the law of God.

Yet for all of this, they were not condemned. They were aware daily that their hearts were deceitful and wicked. They could feel their flesh, their evil nature, still within them. Yet so long as they did not yield to it, so long as they did not give place to Satan, so long as they continued a war against sin, they walked in the Spirit. Their flesh did not have dominion over them. Therefore there was still no condemnation to them who were in Jesus Christ. God was well pleased with their sincere, though imperfect, obedience. They still had confidence toward God, knowing they were His, by the Spirit He had given them.[9]

Babes in Christ know the truth about themselves. They

are thoroughly convinced that sin cleaves to all they do. They are conscious of not fulfilling the perfect law, either in their thoughts, words, or works. They know they do not love the Lord their God with all their mind, soul, and strength. They are aware that they feel a measure of pride and self-will stealing in to mix with their best intentions. This occurs even when they come together in worship to pour out their souls in secret to God, who sees all the purposes and intents of the heart. They are continually ashamed of their wandering thoughts, or of the deadness of their love. Still there is no condemnation to them either from God or from their own heart.

Their consideration of these many faults gives only a deeper sense of always needing the blood sacrifice of Jesus, which speaks to God for them. They are continually thankful for that advocate with the Father, who lives eternally to make intercession for them.

So these lingering imperfections do not drive them away from Him in whom they have their belief. Rather, they drive them closer to Jesus for whom they feel the need every moment. The deeper the sense of this need, the more earnest the desire to walk with Jesus, and feel His presence.

They are not condemned for those sins which are usually called sins of infirmity, namely, involuntary failings. An example of a sin of infirmity is the saying of a thing which we believe to be true when it proves to be false. It is hurting our neighbor without knowing or planning to do so. Such a thing can occur even when we have intended to do that neighbor a good turn.

These deviations from the wholly acceptable and perfect will of God are not sins, nor do they bring any guilt on the conscience of them who are in Christ Jesus. They do not separate God and the believer. They do not intercept the light of His grace. They are in no way inconsistent with the character of walking not after the flesh, but after the Spirit. Finally, there is no condemnation to them for anything whatever which is not in their power to prevent. This applies to acts of both inward and outward nature, whether it be the doing of something or the leaving of something undone. For example, the Lord's Supper is to be administered. You do not participate in the sacrament. Why do you not participate? If you are sick and cannot help missing the service, you are not condemned. There is no guilt because there is no choice. If you are willing to be in the will of God, but are unable to do so, that willingness is accepted just as if you had done that will. A believer may sometimes be grieved because he cannot do what he longs to do. He may cry out in anguish when he is prevented from worshiping God in church. He says, "My soul is athirst for the living God. When shall I get to come into His presence?" He may earnestly desire to witness to others to bring them into the faith. But if he cannot go out to witness, he feels no guilt, no condemnation, no sense of God's displeasure. When he can do this, he gives thanks to God who is his help, and who brings about the circumstance of the action.

There are also sins of surprise. It is more difficult to determine whether or not these separate God and man. An example of them is when one who usually has patience speaks or acts in a manner not consistent with love, because of a sudden or violent temptation. It is not easy to fix a general rule concerning sins of this nature. We cannot say that men are or are not condemned for sins of surprise in general. It seems that whenever a believer is overtaken in a sin of surprise, there is some condemnation, more or less. This condemnation is related to the more-or-less acceptance of it by his will. In proportion that a sinful word, thought, or action is voluntary, so we may understand that God is more or less displeased, and there is more or less guilt upon the soul.

There can be some sins of surprise which bring much guilt and condemnation. In some instances, our being surprised is due to some willful neglect in our spiritual life. The surprise can be due to some laziness or sloth which could have been prevented or shaken off before the temptation came. The believer could have been previously warned either by God or man that temptations are at hand. In spite of this warning, he may say to himself, "I will rest a little longer before confronting this problem." If that person should afterwards fall into sin, though unaware, that unawareness is no excuse. He could have foreseen and shunned the danger. The falling, even by surprise in such an instance as this, is in effect a willful sin. As such, it exposes the sinner to condemnation both from God and his own conscience. On the other hand, there may be sudden assaults which could not be foreseen. They can come from the world, from Satan, or from our own evil hearts.

A believer who is still weak in the faith may fall before such assaults. He may express a degree of anger or think evil of another person without having a willful desire to do those things. In such a case, the Holy Spirit will undoubtedly show him that he has acted foolishly. He would be convinced of having swerved from the perfect law, from the mind which was in Christ. He would be grieved and lovingly ashamed before God. Still he does not come into condemnation. God does not charge him with this sin, but has compassion for him as a father pities his own children. His heart does not condemn him in the midst of that sorrow and shame either. He can still say, "I will trust, and will not be afraid, for the Lord God is my strength and my song, and he has become my salvation."[10]

If there is no condemnation on account of past sins, then why be fearful and of little faith? If your sins have been numberless, why do you care about them now that you are saved through Jesus Christ? Who can accuse you of anything when you are one of God's elect? It is God who saves, so who is it who can condemn you? All the sins you have committed from your first day until now have been forgiven by Jesus. They are driven away as chaff, they are gone, are lost, are swallowed up to be remembered no more. Why should anyone who has been reborn of the Holy Spirit be troubled or afraid of what was done before that new birth? Put away all those fears. You are not called to a spirit of fear. You are called to a spirit of love and of a sound mind. Know your calling. Rejoice in God your Savior. Give thanks to God your Father through Jesus Christ.

Some will say they have committed sin since this new birth. If that is true, then repent. It is necessary to abhor yourself for your sins so that you can repent. It is God himself who has brought you to this point so you can see yourself as you truly are. But you do believe now. You are able to say, "I know my redeemer lives." You can affirm that the life you now live you live by faith in Jesus. That faith still cancels out all that is past. Therefore, there is no condemnation to you. At whatever time you truly believe in the name of Jesus, all your sins to that moment vanish away.

Stand fast in the liberty with which Jesus has made you free. He has once more made you free from the power of sin. He has made you free from the guilt and punishment of sin. Do not become entangled with the yoke of bondage again. Through Jesus, you are free from the devilish bondage of sin, evil desires, evil tempers, evil works, evil words. Such bondage is the most grievous yoke this side of hell. Accept your freedom from the bondage of slavish tormenting fear, guilt, and self-condemnation.

We can wonder about those who claim to abide in Jesus Christ, but walk after the flesh in the world and not after the

Holy Spirit. They are now condemned in their own hearts. If we are condemned in our hearts, our own conscience bears witness that we are guilty. It is God who does this, for He is greater than our heart and knows all things. We cannot deceive Him even if we can deceive ourselves. We cannot claim we were saved once, and this will overcome current sins. We know with the utmost degree of certainty that he who willfully commits sins is of the devil. Therefore, if one remains in sin, his father is Satan. This cannot be denied, because he does the works of his father.

We cannot rely upon vain hopes. We cannot say to ourselves, "Be at peace," when there is no peace. In those times we must cry to God from the depths of the soul. God must be approached as He was at first. As at first, we come again, wretched and poor, sinful, miserable, blind, and naked. There can be no allowance for rest until His pardoning love is received again. There must be a crying out until the backslidings are healed. Prayers to Him are continued until the faith which works by love is received again.

There is no condemnation for any inward sin still remaining to them who walk after the Spirit. They are not guilty of sin as long as they do not give in to it. They are not guilty for sins which cleave to all they do. They do not worry because of ungodliness remaining only in the heart. They do not pine away, because they still come short of the glorious image of God. They know they are not yet perfected because of pride, self-will, and unbelief that cleave to all their words and works. They are not afraid to know all of this evil in their heart. It is important for them to know themselves as they are known by God.

It is the desire of God that a Christian not think more highly of himself then he ought to think. Therefore, his continual prayer to God is, "Show me, God, as my soul can bear it, the depth of my inbred sin." When God hears this prayer, He unveils the heart. When He shows us thoroughly what spirit we have, we must be careful not to despair. We are humbled and abased, but we must not allow our shield of faith to be torn away. We are to see ourselves as less than nothing, and mostly vanity. But still our hearts need not be troubled or afraid. We hold fast knowing we have an advocate with the Father, Jesus Christ, our righteousness. As the heavens are higher than the earth, so His love is higher than all our sins. Therefore, God is merciful to all sinners. Such sinners we are, but God is love, and Jesus has died for us. Therefore, He will withhold nothing which is good from us.

It is good that the whole body of sin which is in us be destroyed. It shall be done. We can be cleansed from all sins of both flesh and spirit. The whole body of sin which has been crucified in us must now be destroyed. Nothing is to remain in our hearts but the pure love of God.

You shall come to love the Lord God with all your soul, heart, mind, and strength. He has promised this, and He is faithful. He will do this work in us. It is your part to patiently continue in the works of faith, and in the labor of love. Stay in cheerful peace, humble confidence, with calm, yet resigned expectation. Earnestly wait until the Lord God shall perform this perfection in you.

Those who are in Christ and walk in the Spirit are not condemned for sins of infirmity or involuntary failings, or anything that they are not able to avoid. But beware that Satan does not gain an advantage because of your faith in Jesus' blood. We remain foolish and weak, blind and ignorant. We are weaker than any words can describe. We are more foolish than we can understand.

None of us knows all the spiritual things which we ought to know. But we need not let all the weakness and folly, or any of the effects of it which are unavoidable, shake our faith.

Nothing can be allowed to disturb our basic trust in God and our peace and joy in the Lord.

The rule which some give as to willful sins is undoubtedly wise and safe if it is applied only to the case of weakness and infirmities. If you have fallen, do not lie there fretting and bemoaning your weaknesses. Meekly say, "Lord, I shall fail every moment unless you uphold me with your hand." Then stand up. Leap and walk. Go on your way. Run with patience the race which is set before you.

A believer does not come into condemnation even though he is surprised into a sin. It grieves the Lord when any believer falls into sin by surprise. Such sin by surprise can be a precious balm if it is not due to any willful neglect on his part. Pour out your heart to God and show Him the trouble. Pray with all your might to Him who is touched by His children's infirmities. Then He will establish, strengthen, and settle the soul. He will strengthen and allow no further falls.

He does not condemn. Why should any believer fear? There is no need of any fear which has torment. Simply love Him who loves you. This additional love will bring more strength. As soon as we love Him with all our hearts, we become perfect and entire, lacking nothing. Wait in peace for the time when the God of peace purifies you completely. Then your whole spirit, soul, and body will be preserved blameless until the coming of Jesus Christ.

From "The First Fruits of the Spirit," *Forty-Four Sermons*, Sermon VIII.

7

Gifts of the Holy Spirit

The nature of the miraculous gifts of the Holy Spirit is taught both by Scripture and the writings of the early church fathers. These fathers wrote after the apostolic age.

The original promise of the gifts of the Holy Spirit was from Jesus. St. Mark records His word, "These signs shall follow them that believe; In my name shall they cast out devils; they shall speak with new tongues; they shall take up serpents, and if they drink any deadly thing, it shall not hurt them; they shall lay hands on the sick, and they shall recover."[1]

A further account was given by St. Peter on the very day that promise was fulfilled. The account of Peter is: "This is that which was spoken of by the prophet Joel; And it shall come to pass in the last days, saith God . . . your sons and your daughters shall prophesy, and your young men shall see visions, and your old men shall dream dreams."[2]

A more complete list of the gifts of the Holy Spirit was given by St. Paul in his first letter to the Corinthians. He wrote: "There are diversities of gifts [*charismata*, the usual scriptural term for the miraculous gifts of the Holy Spirit],

97

but the same Spirit. For to one is given by the Spirit the word of wisdom; to another the word of knowledge by the same Spirit; to another faith by the same Spirit; to another the gifts of healing by the same Spirit; to another the working of [other] miracles; to another prophecy; to another discerning of spirits; to another diverse kinds of tongues; to another the interpretation of tongues. But all these worketh that one and the selfsame Spirit, dividing to every man severally as he will."[3]

Thus, we may observe that the chief charismata, or spiritual gifts, conferred on the apostolic church were: (1) casting out devils; (2) speaking with new tongues; (3) escaping dangers, in which otherwise they might have perished; (4) healing the sick; (5) prophecy, foretelling the things to come; (6) visions; (7) divine dreams; and, (8) discerning of spirits.

Some of them, particularly the gifts of casting out devils and speaking with new tongues, appear to have been designed chiefly to convince Jews and heathens of the power and validity of the gospel. Some were chiefly for the benefit of their fellow Christians, as healing the sick, foretelling of things to come, and the discernment of spirits. All were given to enable Christians who experienced or witnessed them to run with patience the race set before them, through all the storms of persecution, which the most continual prejudice, rage, and malice could raise.

Since that time, some have attempted to prove: (1) no miracles occurred in the early church after the apostolic age; (2) all the early church leaders who claimed that these gifts were still at work were fools or scoundrels, and most of them were both one and the other; (3) no miracles were wrought by Christ or the apostles; and, (4) that they, too, were fools or scoundrels, or both.

I do not agree with them on any of these points. My

reasons are set forth in as free a manner as I can express. To agree with these objections would be to ignore both Scripture and history. The testimony of the church fathers of the first 300 years of the church will be used to prove that the gifts of the Spirit existed after the apostolic age.

You may naturally ask, "Why do you stop there? What reason can you give for this? If you cite miracles before the Roman Empire became Christian, why not afterward?"

I answer that after the empire became Christian, a general corruption of faith and morals infected the Christian church. By that revolution, as St. Jerome says, "The church lost as much of her virtue as it had gained of wealth and power."[4] And this very same reason was given by St. Chrysostom in the words, "There are some who ask, 'Why are not miracles performed still? Why are there no persons who raise the dead and cure diseases?' " To which he replies that it was due to the lack of faith, virtue, and piety in those times.[5] [6]

It does not appear that those extraordinary gifts of the Holy Spirit were common in the church for more than two or three centuries. We seldom hear of them after that fatal period when the Emperor Constantine called himself a Christian. Then he, from a vain imagination of promoting the Christian cause, heaped riches, power, and honor upon Christians in general, but in particular upon the Christian clergy. From that time, the gifts of the Holy Spirit almost totally ceased. Very few instances of this kind were to be found after that.[7]

The cause of this was not (as has been vulgarly supposed) that there was no more need or occasion for them, because all the world had become Christian. This is a miserable mistake. Not a twentieth part of the world was then nominally Christian. The real cause of the loss was that the love of many, almost all the so-called Christians had grown cold. The Christians had no more of the Spirit of Christ than the other heathens. The Son of Man, when He came to examine His church, could hardly find faith on earth. This was the real cause why the extraordinary gifts of the Holy Spirit were no longer to be found in the Christian church after that time. It was because the Christians had turned heathen again, and had only a dead form left.[8]

So, when this faith and holiness were nearly lost, dry, formal, orthodox men began even then to ridicule whatever gifts they did not have themselves. They belittled and discredited all the gifts of the Spirit as either madness or fraud. As a result, the miraculous gifts of the Holy Spirit were soon withdrawn from the early church.[9]

Therefore, to say the miracles never occurred is to say that all who participated in them were either fools or scoundrels. They would be fools for believing miracles occurred if they had not. They would be scoundrels if they reported miracles had occurred if they knew they had not. Claims that the miraculous powers and gifts of the Holy Spirit ended with the apostles is canceled by the testimonies of the early church fathers. Where is the proof they were wrong? Who is to say they were either fools or scoundrels? Without proof, no one can.

Proceed to the testimony of Justin Martyr who wrote about fifty years after the apostles.[10] He wrote, "There are prophetic gifts among us even until now. You may see with us both women and men having gifts from the Spirit of God." He particularly insisted upon casting out devils as the gift that everyone might see with his own eyes.

Irenaeus,[11] who wrote somewhat later, affirms "that all who were truly disciples of Jesus wrought miracles in His name: Some cast out devils; others had visions, or the knowledge of future events; others healed the sick." And as to raising the dead, he declares it to have been frequently performed on necessary occasions by great fasting and the joint supplication of the church. "We hear many," says he, "speaking with all kinds of tongues, and expounding the mysteries of God."

Theophilus, [12]Bishop of Antioch, who lived in the same age, speaks of casting out devils as being common in the church at that time.

Tertullian, [13] who flourished toward the end of the second century, challenges the heathen magistrates to "call before their tribunals any person possessed with a devil. If the evil spirit, when commanded by any Christian, did not confess himself to be a devil, who elsewhere called himself a god, they should take the life of that Christian."

Minutius Felix, [14] supposed to have written in the beginning of the third century, addressing himself to a heathen friend, says, "The greatest part of you know what confessions the demons make concerning themselves, when we expel them out of the bodies of men."

Origen, [15] somewhat younger than Minutius, declares that there remained still the manifest indications of the Holy Spirit. "For the Christians," says he, "cast out devils, perform many cures, foretell things to come. And many have been converted to Christianity by visions. I have seen many examples of this sort."

In another place, he says: "Signs of the Holy Spirit were shown at the beginning of the teaching of Jesus, more were shown after His ascension, but afterwards fewer. However, even now there are still some remains of them with a few, whose souls are cleansed by the Word and [who have] a life conformable to it." Again: "Some," says he, "heal the sick. I myself have seen many so healed of loss of senses, madness, and innumerable other evils which neither men nor devils can cure. And this is done, not by magical arts, but by prayer and certain plain adjurations such as any common Christian may use, for generally common men do things of this kind."

Cyprian, [16] who wrote about the middle of the third century, says, "Beside the visions of the night, even in the daytime innocent children among us are filled with the Holy Spirit, and in ecstasies see and hear and speak those things by which God is pleased to admonish and instruct us." Elsewhere he particularly mentions the casting out of devils, which, says he, "either depart immediately or by degrees, according to the faith of the patient or the grace of him that works the cure."

Arnobius, [17] who is supposed to have written in the year of A.D. 303, tells us, "Christ appears even now to men unpolluted and eminently holy who love Him; whose very name puts evil spirits to flight, strikes their prophets dumb, deprives the soothsayers of the power of answering, and frustrates the acts of arrogant magicians."

Lactantius, [18] who wrote about the same time, speaking of evil spirits, says, "Being adjured by Christians, they retire out of the bodies of men, confess themselves to be demons, and tell their names, even the same which are adored in the temples."

Many have reviewed the gifts along with these ancient testimonies and questioned each of the ancient testimonies. A few of these objections and suspicions are listed below. I have given my answers to them.

First is Irenaeus's statement regarding the raising of the dead. He affirmed, "This was frequently performed on necessary occasions; when, by great fastings and the joint supplication of the church, the spirit of the dead person returned to him, and the man was given back on the prayers of the saints."[19]

The objections are, no instances of this raising of the dead may be found in contemporary heathen literature. Second, the heathens constantly affirmed such a thing was impossible. Third, Theophilus, Bishop of Antioch, could not show anyone who had been raised from the dead when challenged to do so.

My answers are that regarding the silence of heathen historians, it is unlikely they would have related such a fact even if they knew of it. It is equally improbable that they would have known of an instance like this. Remember Lazarus? The heathens would have sought to kill the raised Christian. Thus, such instances would have been kept from them. Also, this miracle was not designed for the conversion of the heathen, but for the good of the church. This was a miracle designed, above all others, to support and confirm the Christians who were daily tortured and slain, but sustained by the hope of obtaining a better resurrection.

The fact that the heathens affirmed that such a thing was impossible is true. To them it was impossible. But is it an incredible thing that God should raise the dead?

That Theophilus could not respond to the challenge has no bearing on Irenaeus's testimony. Irenaeus wrote from France forty years before Theophilus. It is unlikely that any of those raised Frenchmen would have been in Antioch forty years later. Irenaeus did not affirm that this was done in every place and every church. It probably occurred only where circumstances were important enough to require it.

All of these objections, even if they were correct, do not invalidate in any degree the express testimony of Irenaeus. Neither do they prove that none have been raised from the dead since the days of the apostles.[20]

The next gift to be discussed is that of healing of the sick, often exercised by anointing the sick with oil.[21] Such healings were attested to by Irenaeus and Origen. Some objections expressed to these claims are: (1) the oil itself accounted for the healing; (2) they were not cured at all, that the claim for the healing was either false or fraudulent; (3)

heathens pretend to heal also; (4) the heathen "miracles" were also fraudulent; and, (5) diseases thought to be fatal and desperate are often surprisingly healed by themselves without Christian faith.

It is true we do not know the exact boundaries between nature and miracles. It is also true that some diseases heal by themselves. But the thrust of these arguments is to attempt to prove there were never any miraculous healings in the world. Such an argument points to Jesus as well as His followers. It tends to show that if there were never any miraculous cures, Jesus performed none either.

While we do not know the precise bounds between nature and miracles, it does not follow that we cannot be assured that there were miracles of healing. To explain this is simple. I do not know precisely what nature can do toward restoring sight to the blind. However, this I do know. If a man born blind is restored to sight by a word, it is not nature, but a miracle. We have such an account which is well attested.[22] All reasonable men give this account their highest regard.

We can agree that: (1) the heathens themselves had miraculous cures among them; (2) oil by itself may cure some diseases; and, (3) we do not know the bounds of nature. These admissions, however, will not prove that no miraculous cures were performed by either Jesus or His apostles or by those who lived in the following centuries.

The third of the miraculous powers said to have been in the primitive church is that of casting out devils. The testimonies which are listed concerning this are numerous and as plain as words can make them.

The major objections to these testimonies is that there never were any devils cast out at all. To claim these events as something else is a large task. But there is one shorter way to object. Throw the whole matter out at a stroke by proving there never was any devil in the world. Then the whole affair of casting him out could be brought to an end. To do such is to call into question the integrity and wisdom of Jesus.

A weak compromise allows the symptoms, but changes the cause. Thus it is stated, "Those who were said to be possessed of the devil may have been ill of a falling sickness. The symptoms seem nothing less than the ordinary symptoms of epilepsy."

So then it may be asked, were the speeches and confessions of the devils and their answering to questions only the symptoms of ordinary epilepsy?

Because there is no answer to that question, a second hypothesis is presented. These acts must have been a result of contrivance and fraud between the persons involved in the act. Now is not this something extraordinary! Here are men in epileptic fits who are capable of such art and contrivance.

Again proof is lacking. We must always call for the proof. Where is the proof? Instead of proof we have only suppositions. The main supposition is that the early church fathers were either too hasty in giving support to these pretended possessions, or carried away by their zeal to support a delusion which was useful to the Christian cause.

By these objections, Jesus and the apostles are struck with equal force as the primitive fathers. By attempting to show that all who claim this power to be either fools or frauds, Jesus is included. This spoils the whole argument. Thus, the ancient testimonies regarding this gift remain firm and unshaken.

The next miraculous gift was that of prophesying. To many, prophecy includes visions, discovering the secrets of men, foretelling the things to come, and religious and spiritual ecstasies. With regard to this gift, religious excesses are often cited. Tertullian's testimony is suspect because of his association with Montanus. The Montanists were accused of fanaticism and heresy. Thus, all who were associated with them came under suspicion. However, disregarding Tertullian for this reason does not remove the testimony of Cyprian. According to him, "Beside the visions of the night, even in the daytime children among us are filled with the Holy Spirit, and in ecstasies see and hear and speak those things by which God is pleased to admonish and instruct us."

"Now, what can we think," say the critics, "of these strange stories, but that they were partly forged, partly dressed up in this tragic form, to support the discipline of the church in those times of danger and trial?"

We must not forget that it was not Tertullian or Cyprian who first raised the issue in the church. Rather, it was Joel and St. Peter who decreed this gift before Montanus was born. From them came the words, "And in the last days it shall be, God declares, that I will pour out my Spirit upon all flesh, and your sons and your daughters shall prophesy, and your young men shall see visions, and your old men shall dream dreams."[23]

So many of us continue to think that these early accounts are true even in the manner they are related. If any of them are not, Cyprian thought they were, and related them with sincerity of heart. Some still believe that the wisdom of God might in those times of danger and trial work things of this kind for that very purpose, to support the disciplines of the church. And until the critics show the falsehood, or at least the improbability of the gift of prophecy, Cyprian's character stands untainted—not only as a man of sense, but likewise of eminent integrity. Consequently, it is beyond dispute that these miraculous gifts remained in the church after the days of the apostles.

The most controversial miraculous gift of the Holy Spirit is the gift of tongues. This, it is sure, was claimed by the primitive Christians, because Irenaeus says expressly, "We hear many in the church speaking with all kinds of tongues." While saying that many in his day had this gift, he did not have the gift himself.

In denying that this gift continued in the early church after the apostles, some assert, "This was granted only on certain special occasions, and then withdrawn from the apostles themselves, so that in the ordinary course of their ministry they were generally destitute of it."

This and Tertullian's case only proved the truth St. Paul had observed long before. "Do all work miracles? Do all possess gifts of healing? Do all speak with tongues?"[24] No, not even when those gifts were given in the most abundant manner.

Then it is stated that no other church father had made the least claim to the gift of tongues. Perhaps this is true of those whose writings are in existence. At least, it is true for their writings which are now in existence. But what are these in comparison of those which are lost? And how many saints of the first three hundred years of the church left no written account at all? Or at least they left no account which has come into our hands.[25]

Who are those who wrote of speaking in tongues as a particular gift only for the times of the apostles? Show me six ante-Nicene fathers who support the objection, "There is not a single father who ventures to speak of it except as withdrawn from the church." Show me these and I will give up the whole point.

In reviewing the objections to the miraculous gifts, one continues to notice a procedure which leads to many errors. With regard to the past, some take this for granted: "What is not recorded was not done." This is by no means a self-evident axiom. Possibly it is not true. There may be many reasons in the depth and wisdom of God for His doing many things at various times and places which were never recorded at all. Such acts may have been done by either His natural or supernatural power. Indeed, many could have once been recorded with the fullest evidence, but are lost to us now at a distance of hundreds of years.

It is possible that this is the situation in the case before us. Many may have spoken in new tongues of whom there is no record. At least, the record of such are lost in the course of many years. It is not only possible that such records are lost, but it is absolutely certain. You must acknowledge it if you acknowledge the apostles spoke while in strange countries. St. John in Asia Minor, St. Peter in Italy, and the other apostles when in either Parthia, Media, Phygria, or Pamphylia spoke to the natives in their own tongues. Nowhere is there a written record of any particular apostle exercising this gift in any country whatsoever.

To follow the axiom, that something not recorded did not occur, would leave us in a peculiar position. The consequence of such would be a conclusion that the apostles no more spoke in tongues than their successors.

An historical mistake is the statement that this gift has not appeared in an authentic setting since the Reformation. It is a mistake to deny that an authentic appearance of this gift is missing from Christianity.

One well-known instance of new tongues occurred in France among the Huguenots. That movement of the Holy Spirit was put down after much effort by Louis XIV, not by the pen of his scholars, but with the swords and bayonets of his dragoons.[26]

Some would lump all of the miraculous gifts of the Holy Spirit together and judge them all by only one. Thus critics would say, if the gift of tongues is genuine, all the other gifts are genuine. Conversely, if the gift of tongues is not genuine, all the other gifts are not genuine.

Such is not so, but otherwise. The rule in the case is, "All these worketh that one and the selfsame Spirit, dividing to every man severally as he will."[27] So it is to every man, every church, and every collective body of believers. The Holy Spirit divides and endows the gifts as He chooses.

If this is so, there is no particular test for determining the pretensions of all churches. God who works as He will may give the gift of tongues where He gives no other. He may see many reasons for doing so, whether you and I see them or not. Perhaps we have not always known the mind of the Lord, not being of the number of His counselors. On the other hand, He may see good reason to give many other gifts where it is not His will to bestow tongues. This would particularly be so in a church where all are of the same mind and speak the same language.

We have now finished after a fashion what we proposed to do. This was to review the several kinds of gifts claimed to be in the early church and answer the objections to those claims. It is time for every impartial man to calmly consider and judge the testimonies and the objections. By an examination of the material at hand, one may determine whether some miracles of each kind have been wrought in the ancient church after the age of the apostles.

From "Letter to Dr. Conyers Middleton," January 4, 1749, Thomas Jackson, ed., The Letters of The Rev. John Wesley, *(London: The Epworth Press, 1931), vol. 2, p. 312ff.*
This letter was in response to a published criticism of the gifts of the Spirit by Middleton. That work was based upon Jean Daille's "De usu Patrum" (1632). Wesley wrote in his Journal, *"I soon saw what occasion that good man had given to the enemies of God to blaspheme, and that Dr. Middleton*

in particular had largely used that work in order to overthrow the Christian system."

While Wesley's letter was directly in answer to Middleton's criticism, it provides the modern Christian with adequate answers to the criticism of the gifts today.

One such theory is that tongues, prophecy, and knowledge have passed away (1 Cor. 13:8ff) because the "perfect" has come. That "perfect" is said to be the New Testament. All of Wesley's ancient authorities cited in this letter wrote after the books of the New Testament were written. Justin, Irenaeus, Tertullian, Cyprian, and Origen all gave lists of the New Testament books in their writings. From this, it is evident that these gifts continued in the church after the New Testament books were written and used in the church.

Additionally, it is currently taught that demonology, concepts of the devil and demons, came into Judaism after the Babylonian exile from contact with Persian religion. The use of such terms and concepts is excused as the way Jesus and His contemporaries described mental and emotional problems in a pre-scientific era. Wesley quickly saw through this argument. If there were no demons and no devil, Jesus would be either a fool or a fraud for His teachings. If Jesus knew there were no spirits of that nature, He would be a fraud for teaching contrary to His knowledge. If He taught incorrectly, not knowing any better, He would be a fool. Wesley did not believe that Jesus was either a fool or a scoundrel.

8

The Witness of the Holy Spirit

*It is the Spirit himself bearing witness with our spirit that
we are children of God. (Romans 8:16)*

Many men, confused in their understanding, have
misinterpreted this Scripture to the destruction of their
souls. They have mistaken the voice of their imagination for
the witness of the Holy Spirit. The result was that they idly
presumed they were children of God while they were
actually doing the works of the devil.

These are truly and properly fanatics[1] in the worst sense
of the word. It is with great difficulty that they are
convinced of their error, especially if they have been deeply
into it. All efforts to bring them to the knowledge of
themselves are considered "fighting against God." Their
contrary spirit, which they term "contending earnestly for
the faith," removes them from all usual methods of
conviction. In observing this situation, we may as well say,
"Only God can reach them."

The general results of such delusions are not surprising.
Reasonable men, seeing the effects of this delusion, attempt

to avoid falling into the same error. Those laboring to keep a distance from fanaticism often lean toward the other extreme. The result is that they are not apt to believe any who claim to have this witness of the Spirit. Because some have been mistaken about inner voices, they assume all can be mistaken. They are ready to classify as fanatics all who use this abused expression and spiritual concept. They question whether the witness or testimony of the Spirit is the privilege of ordinary Christians. Therefore they are apt to conclude this is one of the extraordinary gifts which belonged only to the apostolic age.

There is no necessity to fall into either one extreme or the other. We may steer a middle course. We may keep a sufficient distance from the spirit of error and fanaticism without denying the gift of God. There is no need to give up this gift and great privilege of His children.

To avoid either of these extremes, we need to consider some questions. First, what is this witness or testimony of our spirit? What is the witness of God's Spirit? How does He bear witness with our spirit that we are the children of God? Next, how is this joint testimony of God's Spirit and our spirit distinguished from the presumptions of a natural mind and the delusions of the devil?

First to be considered is the witness or testimony of our spirit. It must be noted that the biblical text does not speak of the witness of our spirit only. There is a real question if the statement of Paul speaks about our own spirit at all. It is very possible that he is speaking only of the witness of God's Spirit.

In the original text, and in the immediately preceding verse, Paul said, "You have received the Spirit of sonship [adoption]. When we cry, 'Abba, Father,' it is the Spirit himself bearing witness with our spirit that we are children of God."[2] This denotes God's witness that we are His children at the same time He enables us to cry, "Abba, Father."

In saying this about the text at hand, I do not exclude the double witness in the new birth experience. There is both the testimony of God's Spirit and the testimony of the Christian's own spirit that he is a child of God.

With regard to the witness of God's Spirit, numerous texts of Scripture describe the marks of the children of God. These texts are easily understood by those who read them. They have been collected and explained by both ancient and modern writers. If any additional understanding is needed, it may be received by God's ministering through His Word. Meditate on the Scriptures in private, and discuss them with those who have more experience in His ways.

Religion was designed to perfect and not to extinguish holy understanding. Paul affirmed this when he wrote, "Do not be children in your thinking; be babes in evil, but in thinking be mature."[3] Every man who applies those scriptural marks to himself may know whether he is a child of God. Thus, he knows first, "For all who are led by the Spirit of God," into all holy tempers and actions, "are sons of God."[4] He can have the infallible assurance of the holy writ. So, he may conclude, "I am thus led by the Spirit of God; therefore, I am a son of God."

John agreed to all this in the plain declarations of his first epistle. "By this we may be sure that we know him, if we keep his commandments. Whoever keeps his word, in him truly love for God is perfected. By this we may be sure that we are in him. If you know that he is righteous, you may be sure that every one who does right is born of him."[5] "We know that we have passed out of death into life, because we love the brethren. By this we shall know that we are of the truth, and reassure our hearts before him."[6] This is because we love one another, not in word, neither in tongue, but in deed and in truth. "By this we know that we abide in him and he in us, because he has given us of his own Spirit."⁷ "By this we know that he abides in us, by the Spirit which he has given us."⁸

It is highly probable that there never had been any Christian who was further advanced in God's grace than the Apostle John when he wrote the words above. Notwithstanding, his attainment in grace and the knowledge of our Lord Jesus Christ, he applied these marks to himself. John and all the pillars of the church applied these measures to their own souls for the confirmation of their faith.

Yet all this is no more than rational evidence. It is the witness of our spirit, the witness of our reason and understanding. Those who have these marks are the children of God. We who have these marks are children of God.

There is a question that still remains. How does it show that we have these marks? Or, how does it show that we love God and our neighbor? How does it show that we keep God's commandments? The meaning of this question is, how does it appear to ourselves that we keep these commandments? We are not to be concerned about how we appear to others in this matter.

This question can be answered with similar questions. How does it appear that you are alive? How do you know that you are now at ease and not in pain? You are immediately conscious of these things. By the same immediate consciousness you can know that your soul is alive to God. You can tell if you have a meek and quiet spirit free from the pain of proud wrath.

By the same means, you surely will perceive love, rejoicing, and delight in God when you experience these feelings. By the same means you can be assured you love your neighbor as yourself. If you have kindly affections toward all mankind, you will know it. You will know if you are full of gentleness and long-suffering.

The outward marks of the keeping of these commandments is also apparent to you. Your conscience speaks to you daily. Do you utter God's name only in seriousness and reverence? Do you remember the Sabbath and keep it holy? Do you honor your father and mother? Do you treat all others as you would have them treat you? Do you control and direct your body as the temple of the Holy Spirit? When you eat and drink, are you temperate about it? Do you do every act of your life to the glory of God?

Now this is properly the testimony of our own spirit. God has given us a conscience to lead us to holiness of heart. It is to keep us holy in conversation. It is a consciousness of having received the Spirit of adoption. Through this Spirit, we express emotions belonging to His adopted children, as are listed in the Word of God.

Thus, we have a loving heart toward God and all mankind. We hang upon God our Father in loving confidence. We desire nothing but Him. We can cast all our cares upon Him. We can embrace all other humans with tender affection. The result is that we are ready to lay down our lives for our brothers, as Christ laid down His life for us.

From this, we are conscious that we are inwardly conformed to the image of Jesus by the Holy Spirit. We walk before God in justice, mercy, and truth, doing the things which are pleasing in His sight.

But what is the testimony of God's Spirit which is always added to this? How does He bear witness with our spirit that we are the children of God? It is hard to find words from man's limited language to explain the deep things of God. Indeed, there are no words which will adequately express what the children of God experience. Within these limitations, one might say the testimony of the Holy Spirit is an inward impression on the soul. The Spirit directly witnesses to our spirit that we are His children. We are assured that Jesus has loved us and given His life for us. We know that our sins are forgiven and forgotten. Faith becomes personal—I, even I, am reconciled to God.

This testimony of God's Spirit must come before the testimony of our own spirit. This is evident by the fact that we must be holy of heart and holy in life before we can be aware that we are so. We must be inwardly and outwardly holy before we can come to believe that we are holy. It is a fact that we must love God before we can be holy at all. Love of God is the root of all holiness. Now we cannot love God until we know He loves us. "We love, because he first loved us."[9] We cannot know His pardoning love to us, until His Spirit witnesses to it in our spirit. So it is evident the testimony of His Spirit must precede our love of God and all holiness. Consequently, the witness of the Holy Spirit to our spirit precedes our inward consciousness of it and the testimony of our spirit concerning it.

At the moment when the Holy Spirit witnesses to our spirit about these things, we love God because He has loved us. Then for His sake we love our brother also. We know all of these things within ourselves, because we "know the things that are freely given to us by God."[10] We know that we are of God. This is the testimony of our own spirit. Joined with the testimony of God's Spirit, it affirms that we are children of God. As long as we continue to love God and keep His commandments, we remain His children.

Nothing can be said about the work of our spirit which tends to limit the work of God's Holy Spirit. It is He that works in us everything that is good. His Spirit also shines upon His work, clearly showing us what He has done. This is one great purpose of our receiving the Holy Spirit. Paul was affirming this fact when he wrote, "that we might know the things that are freely given to us of God." His Spirit strengthens the testimony of our conscience, touching our "simplicity and godly sincerity."[11] The Holy Spirit allows us to understand in a fuller and stronger light the things we do which please Him.

Many will seek a clearer explanation of the Spirit's witness to our sonship. "How does the Holy Spirit bear witness with our spirit that we are the children of God? How can this witness remove all doubt and be an evidence of the reality of our sonship?" The answers are clear.

First, as to the witness of our spirit, the soul perceives its feelings. The soul knows when it loves, delights, and rejoices in God as when it loves and delights in anything on earth. It can no more doubt whether it loves, delights, and rejoices than doubt whether it exists.

He who loves God is He who delights and rejoices in Him. He loves God with a humble joy, a holy delight, and an obedient love. It is he who is a child of God. A Christian who experiences these feelings toward God can in no way doubt his being a child of God. He has the proof of the Scriptures and the inward experience. This combination of testimony makes a proof which is self-evident. Thus the proof of our sonship is manifested in our hearts by an intimated conviction which is beyond all doubt.

How this is done cannot be explained or understood. Such knowledge is beyond all of us. The wind blows, and we hear the sound of it. We cannot tell from where it comes, or to where it goes.[12] We cannot know the secret feelings of each other. In the same manner, no one knows the secret things of God, except God himself.

This much we can know. God, by His Holy Spirit, gives a believer a testimony of his adoption as a child of God. While this testimony is present in a man's soul, he can no more doubt the reality of it than he can stand in sunshine and doubt the sun.

This joint testimony of our adoption as sons of God can be distinguished from mistaken hopes. It differs from presumptions of the natural mind and delusions from the devil. It is important for all to understand these differences. An error here results in deception of the soul. Such errors can have fatal consequences. Those making these mistakes seldom discover the mistake until it is too late to correct it.

First, how can presumptions of the natural mind be avoided? It is certain that one who has never been convicted of sin is prone to this error. He is caught in self flattery, always ready to think more highly of himself than he ought. This is especially so in spiritual things. It is not strange to see a worldly egotist also become a spiritual egotist. When he hears of the privilege Christians have as sons of God, he soon persuades himself that he has the Holy Spirit, too. There are many instances of this around us. This same error has occurred throughout history.

The Scriptures have many marks to help us distinguish truth from presumption. The Scriptures describe and outline the circumstances which go before, which accompany, and which follow the new birth. Anyone who reads the Word of God will not need to be confused. He will see so wide a difference between the pretender and the genuine Christian that there will be no danger of confusing one with the other. Anyone who presumes to have the gift of the Holy Spirit may surely know the truth, if he desires to know. Quickly, he can see that he has been badly deluded, allowing himself to believe a lie. A little reflection on these scriptural marks surrounding the circumstance of the new birth give this proof.

The Scripture describes repentance, or conviction of sin, as constantly going before the witness of pardon. "Repent, for the kingdom of heaven is at hand."[13] "Repent, and believe in the gospel."[14] "Repent, and be baptized every one of you in the name of Jesus Christ for the remission of sins."[15] "Repent ye therefore, and be converted that your sins may be blotted out."[16] In conformity to this, the historical church continually places repentance before pardon, or the witness of it. So the church has confessed, "He pardons and absolves all them that truly repent and absolutely believe His holy gospel." Also, "Almighty God . . . has promised forgiveness of sins to all them who, with hearty repentance and true faith, turn unto Him."

Anyone who has never known a broken and contrite heart is a stranger to this true repentance. The "remembrance of his sins" has never been "grievous to him." Their burden has never been intolerable. If the unrepentant person has repeated those words, he never meant what he said. He merely paid a compliment to God. For this reason alone, he can know that he is yet to experience the real knowledge of the Son of God.

Next, the Scriptures described the experience of being born of God which must precede the witness that we are His children. This new birth is a vast and mighty change from darkness to light. It is a change from the power of Satan unto God. It is a resurrection from the dead—a passing from darkness into light. Thus Paul wrote to the Ephesians, "You he made alive, when you were dead through the trespasses and sins in which you once walked. Even when we were dead through our trespasses, [God] made us alive together with Christ, and raised us up with him, and made us sit with him in the heavenly places in Christ Jesus.[17]

What does he who has never repented know about this? He has never had such a change as this. He is altogether unacquainted with such a thing. He does not even understand this language. He simply says that he was always a Christian. He who knows of no time when he even needed such a change may know that he is not born again, born of the Spirit. He has never known God. He has mistaken the voice of nature for the voice of God.

Present marks, disregarding past experiences, will distinguish a child of God from a self-deceiver. The Scriptures describe that joy in the Lord which accompanies the witness of the Holy Spirit. Such joy is a humble joy, which makes the saved sinner cry out, "Now that my eyes see, I abhor my past life. I am the lowest of all sinners."

Wherever that lowliness is, there is meekness, patience, gentleness, and long-suffering. There is a soft yielding spirit. The forgiven child of God has mildness and sweetness, a tenderness of soul which words cannot express.

Now compare that supposed testimony of the Spirit in the presumptuous man. Just the reverse is in him. The more confident he is of the favor of God, the more he is self-exalting, the more haughty and assuming is his behavior. The stronger witness he imagines himself to have, the more overbearing he is to all around him. Such a person is incapable of receiving any reproof, and more impatient of contradiction. Instead of being meek, gentle, teachable, and "swift to hear, slow to speak," he is the contrary. He is not ready to learn from anyone. He is foul and vehement in his temper and eager in his conversation. There can be a kind of fierceness in his air and manner of speaking. His whole deportment is as if he were going to take matters out of God's hands and devour the adversaries by himself.

The Scriptures teach of one more sign of the witness of the Spirit. "This is the love of God, that we keep his commandments."[18] Jesus himself said, "He who has my commandments and keeps them, he it is who loves me."[19] Love rejoices in obedience, in doing at every point whatever is acceptable to God. A true lover of God hurries to do His will on earth, as it is done in heaven.

Is this the character of the pretender to the love of God? Does this obedience mark his life? No. His "love" gives him a liberty to disobey—to break, not keep the commandments of God. Perhaps when he was in fear of God's punishment, he made an effort to do His will. Now, looking at himself as not under the law, he thinks that he is no longer required to observe it. He is less zealous of good works. He is less careful about abstaining from evil. He is less careful over his own heart and tongue. He is less concerned about denying himself and taking up his cross daily.

In a word, the whole form of his life is changed since he believes himself to be at liberty. He is no longer directing himself to godliness. He does not wrestle with the world and Satan, enduring hardships while agonizing to enter into the kingdom of God at the straight gate. He believes he has found an easier way to heaven. It is a broad, smooth, flowery path, in which he can say to himself, "Take it easy. Eat, drink, and be merry."

It follows with undeniable evidence that he has not the true testimony of his own spirit. He cannot be aware of having spiritual marks which he does not have. He has no meekness, lowliness, and obedience. Because the Holy Spirit cannot witness to a lie, He does not testify that he is a child of God. Because he does not have this Spirit of adoption, he is manifestly a child of the devil.

Know yourself and do not be a miserable self-deceiver. If you are confident of being a child of God, you say that you have the witness in yourself. Can you defy all your enemies? Are you being weighed in the spiritual scale of God and found wanting? The Word of God tries your soul and finds if it is false. If you are not gentle and meek, your joy is worth nothing. It cannot be the joy of the Lord. If you do not keep the commandments, you do not love Him. If not, you do not have the Holy Spirit. Under those circumstances, it is certain and evident by the Scriptures that the Holy Spirit does not bear witness to your spirit that you are a child of God. If you are not, ask Him to remove the scales from your spiritual eyes. Ask that you may know yourself as you are known by God. Ask to receive the sentence of death so you can experience the forgiveness that raises the dead. Hunger to hear His voice say to your spirit, "Be of good cheer. Your sins are forgiven. Your faith has made you whole."

How may one who has the real witness in himself know it from presumption? How do you distinguish day from night? There is an inherent, obvious, essential difference between the one and the other. You may see this difference immediately when you seek to know. As there is a difference between worldly darkness and light, so is there between spiritual darkness and light. When the light of righteousness, the Spirit of God, shines in our soul, we know it. There is an inherent, essential difference between that experience, and the light which arises from our own hope. This difference is immediately and directly perceived. It is like nothing ever known before.

A demand for a more minute and philosophical account of this distinction can never be met. Not even those with the deepest knowledge of God can define the criteria or intrinsic marks of the voice of God. Even Paul, in trial before Agrippa, did not attempt to explain this mystery. Yet when Paul heard the voice of God, he knew that it was the voice of God. Who can explain just how he knew it? Neither man nor angel can explain it.

But to answer more directly, God must be able to make His voice known. When He says, "Your sins are forgiven," He must be willing to have His voice known. Otherwise, He would speak in vain. God is able to forgive. Whatever He wills is accomplished. He accomplishes this to the extent that the forgiven person is absolutely assured of the forgiveness. Still, having heard and been assured that it is the voice of God, a man cannot explain how he knows. God does not expect him to explain. If God did, He would give the means of the explanation.

If there were any natural medium or method to prove the things of God to the inexperienced, then natural men could know the mysteries of God. Such is contrary to the will of God. The Apostle Paul taught that "he is not able to understand them [the gifts of the Spirit of God], because they are spiritually discerned" [20] by the spiritual senses which the natural man does not have.

Pushing the inquiry to the specifically personal level, we ask, "How shall I know that my spiritual senses are proper? How am I assured that this is not my situation, that I mistake my own voice for that of the Holy Spirit?"

Your good conscience toward God gives the answer. The fruits which He has wrought in your spirit gives testimony to the Spirit of God. By these, you can know that you are not in delusion and have not deceived your own soul. The immediate fruits of the Spirit, ruling in the heart, are love, joy, peace, mercy, humbleness of mind, meekness, gentleness, and long-suffering. The outward fruits are the doing of good to all men and avoiding the doing of evil to any. It is walking in the light with a zealous, uniform obedience to all the commandments of God.

The same fruits can distinguish the voice of the Holy Spirit from any delusion of the devil. Satan's proud spirit will not allow you to be humble before God. He neither can, nor will, soften your heart toward an earnest mourning for God. He cannot turn you into a child's love for the Father.

It is not Satan that enables you to love your neighbor. He will not allow you to put on meekness, gentleness, patience, temperance, and the whole armor of God. He will never be a destroyer of his own work—sin.

It is only Jesus who comes to destroy the works of the devil. As surely as there is holiness from God, and sin from Satan, surely you have the witness in yourself as to whom you belong—Satan or God.

When you have the sure witness of God's Spirit to your spirit, you may say, "Thanks be to God for His unspeakable gift! Thanks to God who allows me to know in whom I have believed. He lets me know that it is He who sent forth the Spirit of Jesus into my heart crying, 'Abba, Father.' Even now the Holy Spirit is bearing witness to my spirit that I am a child of God."

See that both your mouth and your life show forth His praise. He sealed you for His own. Glorify Him in your body and spirit, which are His. If you have this hope in yourself, purify yourself as He is pure. While you behold what manner of love God the Father has given you, that you can be a child of God, cleanse yourself. Put away all filthiness of flesh and spirit, perfecting holiness in the fear of God. Let all your thoughts, words, and works be a spiritual sacrifice. Make them holy and acceptable to God through Jesus Christ!

When this is done, the Holy Spirit will fully witness to our spirits that we are forgiven and adopted as children of God. No doubt remains.

From "The Witness of the Spirit," *Forty-Four Sermons,* Sermon X.

9

The Witness of Our Own Spirit

For our rejoicing is this, the testimony of our conscience, that in simplicity and godly sincerity, not with fleshly wisdom, but by the grace of God, we have had our conversation in the world. (2 Cor. 1:12, KJV)

As God's holy Spirit witnesses to our spirit, our spirit also witnesses to God. So the voice of every true believer can echo Paul's words written to the Corinthians. They can affirm Jesus' words: "He who follows me will not walk in darkness."[1]

While the Christian has this light, he rejoices in it. He that has received the Lord Jesus Christ, so walks in Him. While he walks in Him, the exhortation of Paul takes place in his soul. The affirmation of the soul is daily: "Rejoice in the Lord always; again I will say rejoice."[2]

We must consider the foundation and nature of Christian joy. We do not want to build our house on sand, but upon the rock, Jesus Christ. Built upon rock, our house will stand when the storms come, and we will continue to have Christian joy.

125

We know, in general, that Christian peace is a happy peace and a calm satisfaction of spirit. It comes from our conscience as described by Paul. For the fullest understanding of this joy, it is necessary to study Paul's complete statement about our joy. Key words are both conscience and testimony. When we have this godly testimony, we can rejoice always.

First we need to have an understanding of conscience. Everyone uses this word, but what does it mean? It seems that it should not be difficult to discover. Many books have been written on the subject. The words of both ancient and modern languages have been sifted in order to explain it. But the results of this attention have not been too enlightening.

God made us thinking beings. We are capable of both perceiving the present and reflecting on the past. In particular, we are capable of understanding whatever occurs in our hearts and lives. We can know what we feel or do. We can know such things while they are occurring and after they are past. This is what we mean when we describe ourselves as conscious beings. We mean man has a consciousness or inward perception. This consciousness is of things present and past which relate to the self. This consciousness includes an awareness of both feelings and actions.

What we usually term conscience includes more than this. We understand that conscience has a larger responsibility than mere memory or awareness. Its main business is to excuse or accuse, to approve or disapprove, to acquit or condemn.

Modern writers would like to change the meaning of the term conscience to moral sense or ethics. The older word is preferable because it is more familiar. It is more easily understood and scriptural. It is the word which God has chosen to give us through the Bible.

According to the meaning usually employed in the Bible, particularly by Paul, conscience is from God. It is a faculty or power implanted by God in every person. Through it, man perceives what is right or wrong in his own heart or life, emotions, thoughts, words, and actions.

There are rules by which men judge right and wrong. These rules direct the conscience, also. Paul wrote that the rule of the heathen is written in his heart. Having no outward law, heathens are a law unto themselves. Their consciences bear witness whether they walk by the rule or not. Their thoughts accuse, excuse, acquit, and defend them.[3]

For Christians, the rule of right and wrong is the Word of God—the Bible. All that the prophets and holy men of old wrote for us, as they were moved by the Holy Spirit, applies. All Scripture, because it was given by the inspiration of God, is profitable for doctrine. It can teach the whole will of God. It can reprove those who live contrary to God's will and correct error. It instructs and trains us in righteousness.[4]

The Bible is a lantern for a Christian's travel. It lights all his paths. This alone is his rule of right or wrong. It shows him what is good or evil. He believes nothing good, but what is taught there, either directly or by plain consequence. He believes nothing to be evil, but what the Word forbids, either by words or by undeniable inference. Whatever the Scripture neither forbids nor requires is neutral. Those matters are believed to be neither good nor evil. The Bible is what directs the Christian's conscience in all things.

If his conscience is in fact so directed, he always has a clear conscience toward God. A good conscience is one which is without offense. Thus Paul could say, "I have lived before God in all good conscience up to this day."[5] At another time Paul said, "So I always take pains to have a clear conscience toward God and toward men."[6]

To keep a clear conscience towards God, we need a right understanding of the Word of God. We must know His holy, acceptable, and perfect will concerning us as it is revealed in the Bible. It is impossible to walk by a rule if the meaning of the rule is unknown.

There is a second requirement for a clear conscience. We must have a knowledge of ourselves which few have attained. We need a true knowledge of both our hearts and lives, of our inward emotions and outward conversation. If we do not know ourselves, we cannot compare ourselves to God's rules.

Another requirement for a clear conscience before God is an agreement. Our lives and thoughts must be in agreement with God's Word. Without this agreement, our conscience can only be said to be an evil conscience.

Next, there must be an inward perception of this agreement. We must always be aware and have an inward consciousness that our lives conform with God's will. It is this inward awareness which we term a good conscience. It is "a clear conscience (one void of offense) toward God and toward men."

Anyone who desires a conscience void of offense must lay the proper foundation. Let him remember no man can lay any other foundation than that which is laid in Jesus Christ. Let him also be aware that no one builds upon Jesus except through a living faith. No man is a partaker of Christ until he can clearly testify, "The life I now live in the flesh, I live by faith in the Son of God."[7] My life is in Him who is now revealed in my heart. I know Him who loved me and gave himself for me.

Living faith is that evidence, that conviction, that demonstration of things invisible. It is faith by which the eyes of our understanding are opened. Through this living faith, divine light is poured in, and we see the wonderful things of God's law. We see the excellency and the purity of it. Through faith we perceive the height, depth, length, and breadth of every commandment contained in it. It is by this faith that, beholding the light of the glory of God in Jesus, we perceive as in a mirror all that is within ourselves. We come to see the inmost motions of our souls, and the love of God is shed abroad in our hearts. This is the faith which allows us to love one another as Christ loved us. By this is that generous promise of God now fulfilled, "I will put my laws into their minds and write them on their hearts."[8] By this, an entire agreement with His holy and perfect laws is produced in our souls. All of our thoughts are brought into captivity for obedience to Christ.

As an evil tree cannot bring forth good fruit, so a good tree cannot bring forth evil fruit. So it is that both the heart and life of a believer thoroughly conform to the rule of God's commandments. In awareness of this, the Christian gives the glory to God. He can then identify with Paul and understand his writings. He shares in Paul's rejoicing. "This is our rejoicing, the testimony of our conscience, that in simplicity and godly sincerity, not with fleshly wisdom, but by the grace of God, we have had our conversation [association] with the world."

"We have had our conversation" is a curious expression. In the original Greek, Paul expresses it with the single word *anastrepho*. The meaning of the word is broad and includes every inward as well as outward circumstance relating to our body and soul. It includes every motion of our heart, tongue, hands, and bodily members. It extends to all our actions and words. It covers the employment of all our powers and faculties. It includes the manner of using every talent we have received, with respect either to God or man.

We have had our conversation in the world, even in the world of the ungodly. This is a world which includes not only the children of God, but the children of the devil. It includes all those who lie in wickedness (literally, in the wicked one, Satan himself).

How completely the world is impregnated with spirits. As our God is good, and does good, so does Satan and all his children, who are evil, do evil to God's children. Like their father, Satan, they are always seeking whom they may destroy. They use fraud or force, secret wiles or open violence to destroy those who are not of the world. They continually war against our souls with both old and new weapons. Using devices of every kind, they labor to bring Christians into the snare of the devil. The broad and easy road which leads to destruction is their way.

Christians live in such a world, in simplicity and godly sincerity. Simplicity is that which Jesus recommends under the name of a "single eye." He taught, "The light of the body is the eye: if therefore thine eye be single, thy whole body shall be full of light."[9] If your intention is single—to do only what God wills—all your actions and conversations shall be full of light. The Christian is full of the light of heaven, love, peace, and joy in the Holy Spirit.

With this single eye fixed upon God, we become simple of heart. Simplicity comes from aiming at God alone in all things The single eye knows God as our portion, our strength, our happiness, our exceeding great reward, our all, in time and eternity. This simplicity comes when a steady view, a single intention of promoting His glory, of doing and suffering His blessed will, runs through our whole soul and fills our heart. This becomes the constant spring of all our thoughts, desires, and purposes.

We also have our conversation in the world in godly sincerity. The difference between simplicity and sincerity is clear. Simplicity is related to the intention, and sincerity to the execution of the intention. This sincerity relates not only to our words, but to our whole conversation, as conversation has been described. It cannot be understood here in the narrower sense Paul sometimes used. At times Paul used the term sincerity to express avoiding guile, craft, and dissimulation. But here he has a more extensive meaning—to speak and do all to the glory of God. Through this sincerity, all our actions flow in an even stream. We actually move straight toward God continually. We always walk steadily on the highway of holiness, in the paths of justice, mercy, and truth.

Paul calls this sincerity godly sincerity, or the sincerity of God. We cannot confuse it with the sincerity of the heathens. They also have a kind of sincerity for which they profess great admiration. Believer's sincerity denotes the object and the end of every Christian virtue as that which tends toward God. Anything which does not ultimately tend toward God sinks down to the beggarly elements of the world. By naming it the sincerity of God, Paul identifies the creator of it. It, being a godly sincerity, comes from the Father of light, from whom every good and perfect gift comes. This understanding is more clearly declared in the following words, "Not with fleshly wisdom, but by the grace of God."

"Not with fleshly wisdom" is Paul's reminder to us of the conditions of simplicity and sincerity. It is as if he had said, "We cannot converse in the world by any natural strength or understanding." We cannot gain this simplicity or practice this sincerity by the effects of good sense, good nature, or good breeding. It overshoots our courage and resolution, as well as our precepts of philosophy. The power of custom is not able to train us for it. The best rules of human education will not equip us. Paul could never attain this regardless of the advantages he enjoyed in the flesh. It was unattainable while he was in his natural state pursuing it only by fleshly, natural wisdom.

Surely if any man could attain this simplicity by wisdom, Paul would have. We can hardly conceive of anyone who was more favored with the gifts of both nature and education. Besides his natural abilities, probably inferior to none, he studied at the University of Tarsus and at the feet of the great teacher Gamaliel. Paul also had all the advantages of religious education. Being a Pharisee, the son of a Pharisee, he had been trained in that very strict and straight sect from his earliest age. He had gained more from this than many others who were of his same age. Paul was more zealous for all things which he thought would please God. He always sought to be blameless in all matters touching on the righteousness of the law. But from all this effort and advantage, Paul could not attain simplicity and godly sincerity. It was all lost labor. From a deep piercing sense of this, he was at length constrained to cry out, "But what things were gain to me, those I counted loss for Christ. Yea, doubtless, and I count all things but loss for the excellency of the knowledge of Christ Jesus my Lord."[10]

He could never attain simplicity except by the "excellent knowledge of Jesus Christ," and then only by the grace of God. The expression "by the grace of God" is sometimes understood to be the love of God, the free unmerited mercy by which any sinner, through the merits of Jesus, is reconciled to God. Here it means that power of God, the Holy Spirit, who works in us, both to will and to do His pleasure. As soon as God's grace in the former sense of pardoning love is manifested to us, His grace in the latter sense is given. The power of the Holy Spirit makes it possible for us to perform, through grace, what was impossible to man. Now we can order our conversation correctly. We can do all things in the light and power of that love through Christ who strengthens us. We now have the testimony of our conscience which we could never have by fleshly wisdom. Now "in simplicity and godly sincerity we have our conversation in the world."

This is the proper ground of Christian joy. We may now readily understand how he who has this testimony in himself can rejoice forever. He may say, "My soul magnifies the Lord and my spirit rejoices in God my Savior. I rejoice in Him, whose love and mercy I do not merit, who has called me to salvation. Because of this, I now stand through His power. I rejoice because His Holy Spirit bears witness to my spirit that I have been bought with the blood of Jesus. By that atonement and my believing in Him, I am a member of Christ, a child of God, and an heir to the kingdom of heaven."

We rejoice because the sense of God's love to us has caused us to love Him, to love for His sake every person whom He has made. We rejoice because He allows us to feel in ourselves the mind which was in Jesus. That mind gives us simplicity, a single eye to Him in every motion of our hearts. It gives us the power to fix the loving eye of the soul on Him who loved us and gave himself for us. It motivates us to aim at Him alone, at His glorious will, in all we speak, think, or do. It attracts us toward purity, whereby we desire nothing more in life but God. Through His Spirit we can crucify the flesh and its affections and lusts, setting our affections on things above, not on things of the earth. This new love molds us into holiness, a recovery of His image with a renewal of soul in His likeness. Now there can be godly sincerity directing all our words and works conducive to His glory. In this we also can and do rejoice, because our consciences witness in the Holy Spirit by the light that He continually pours in upon it, that we walk worthy to the vocation to which we are called. We abstain from all appearance of evil, fleeing from sin as from a serpent.

As we have opportunity, we do all possible good to all men

as we follow in our Lord's footsteps and do what is acceptable in His sight. We rejoice because we both see and feel, through the inspiration of the Holy Spirit, that all our works are wrought in Him. We know that it is He who works the works in us. We rejoice in seeing through the light of God that shines in our hearts. We rejoice for the power we have to walk in His ways. We rejoice knowing that through His grace, we never need to turn out of His way, either to the right hand or to the left.

This is the foundation and nature of that joy in which a Christian can rejoice forever. It is easy to see that this is not a natural joy. It does not arise from any natural cause. No sudden flow of spirits yields it. Some may receive a transient joy from other spirits, but the Christian rejoices always. His joy cannot be due to bodily health or ease; it does not come because of strength and soundness of body. Christian joy is equally strong in sickness and pain. Perhaps it is even stronger under adversity. Many Christians have never experienced any joy that can be compared with the joy of the soul when the body was almost worn out with pain or consumed with illness.

Least of all can this joy be ascribed to outward prosperity, to the favor of others, or an abundance of worldly goods. It is when faith has been under trial by all sorts of afflictions that Christians rejoice in the unseen God they love with unspeakable joy. Never did men rejoice like those early Christians who were treated as the filth and offscouring of the world. They wandered to and fro, often in the need of mere necessities. Often they were cold and hungry without proper clothing. They experienced cruel mockings and imprisonments. They were willing to give up their lives to finish their existence in joy.

These considerations also infer that the joy of a true Christian does not arise from any deadness or blindness of his conscience. It is not due to his being unable to know good from bad. Far from it! He did not even know this joy until he became aware of the difference between good and evil. He could not have this joy until his spiritual senses were re-created to discern spiritual good and evil. After that re-creation, his soul's eye did not dim. He was more sharp-sighted than before. He developed a quick perception of things to the amazement of natural man.

As a speck is visible in the sunshine, every speck of sin is visible to him who is walking in the light of the Son. The Christian never again closes the eye of his conscience. Such spiritual sleep has left him forever. His soul is always awake. He is always standing on the watchtower listening for what his Lord will say to him. In this he is always rejoicing, in the seeing Him who is invisible.

Christian joy does not arise from any dullness or callousness of the conscience. It is true that a kind of joy may result from this in the lives of those whose hearts are spiritually darkened. They have callous, unfeeling hearts, dull of sense and lacking understanding. Because of senselessness and unfeeling hearts, they may rejoice even while committing sin. This way of life they call liberty. It is not liberty, but drunkenness of soul, a fatal numbness of spirit with a stupid insensibility to the conscience. On the contrary, the Christian has the most exquisite sensibility. He could have never even conceived of such sensibility before his regeneration. He never had such tenderness of conscience until the love of God captured his heart.

It is also his glory and joy that God has heard his daily prayer:

> O that my tender soul might fly
> The first abhorr'd approach of ill;
> Quick as the apple of an eye,
> The slightest touch of sin to feel.[11]

Christian joy, then, is joy in obedience. It is joy in loving God and keeping His commandments. Yet the commandments are not kept as only fulfilling the terms of a covenant of works. No such works or righteousness of ours is able to procure pardon and acceptance with God. Joy comes from being already pardoned and accepted, through the mercy of God in Christ Jesus. Obedience is not rendered as if it would purchase spiritual life and acquittal from the death of sin, which we already have through the grace of God. He has quickened us who were already dead in sins, and now we are alive to God through Jesus Christ our Lord.

Now we rejoice in knowing that being saved through His grace, we have not received that grace in vain. Now that God has freely reconciled us to himself, through the sacrifice of Jesus alone, we have the strength to live our lives in the way of His commandments. God has girded us with the strength for spiritual war, and we gladly fight the good fight of faith. We rejoice through Him who lives in our hearts by faith and lay hold of eternal life.

This is our rejoicing: As our Father works here, we also work the works of God. We do this not by our own might or wisdom, but through the power of the Holy Spirit, freely given in Christ Jesus.

May He always work in us what is pleasing in His sight. To Him the praise be given for ever and ever.

From "The Witness of Our Own Spirit," *Forty-Four Sermons*, Sermon XI.

10

Dedication

Turn in the account of your stewardship, for you can no longer be steward. (Luke 16:2)

Various analogies of the relation which man has to God are given in the Bible. As a sinner, a fallen creature, man is represented as a debtor to God. He is also considered a servant, in that Jesus was given that title while He was on earth. Jesus took upon himself the form of servant, being made in the likeness of man.

No title more correctly represents the present state of man than that of a steward, because Jesus frequently called man a steward. There is a particular suitability in this representation, because a steward is a servant of a particular kind.

We need to inquire in what respect we are God's stewards. We need to observe that when He requires our souls of us, we can no longer be stewards; we will be required to give an account of our stewardship.

As stewards, we are responsible to God for using wisely all that God has given us. A debtor is required to return what he has borrowed when the time of repayment comes and is at liberty to use it as he pleases. This is not so with a steward. A steward must use what he has been given only as the owner pleases. He has no right to dispose of anything except by the will of the owner. Not being the proprietor of those things entrusted to him, a steward must dispose of them as the owner orders.

This is exactly the case of every man with relation to God. We are not at liberty to use as we please what God has put in our hands, but only as He pleases. God alone is the owner of heaven and earth and the Lord of every creature. We have no right to dispose of anything we have except according to His will, and we must follow the specific directions He has given to us in His Word, the Bible.

Our souls, our bodies, our goods, our immortal spirits, and whatever talents we have, are entrusted to us on this condition. Thus, we are stewards of our understanding, imagination, will, and all the other affections. Love, hatred, joy, sorrow, desire, aversion, hope, and fear are emotions for which we are responsible because they are reactions of the soul. Paul seems to include all of these when he says, "The peace of God, which passes all understanding, will keep your hearts and your minds."[1] Paul's word for mind, *noema*, might better be translated as thoughts. We need to understand the word in its most extensive sense, which includes every perception of the mind, whether active or passive.

In doing God's will, we most effectually bring about our own happiness—both in time and eternity. So we are to use our understanding, imagination, and our memory wholly to the glory of God. Our will is to be given completely to Him. All our efforts and affections are to be regulated as God directs. We are to love and hate, rejoice and grieve, desire and shun, hope and fear, according to what God prescribes.

We are His, and It is He whom we are to serve in all things. Even our thoughts are not our own. We are accountable to God for every deliberate motion of our mind. God has entrusted us with our bodies as well as with our minds. We are but stewards of these exquisite machines, along with all the powers and members of them. He has entrusted us with the organs of sense, sight, hearing, and all the rest. None of them are given to us as our own, to be used according to our own will. None of them are lent to us to be used as we please, even just for a while. We have received these on very express terms. As long as our senses are with us, we must employ them according to the will of God.

It is on these same terms that He gives us the talent of speech. Men were given tongues to praise God. They are to be employed only in glorifying God. Nothing is more ungrateful or absurd than to think that our tongues are our own. They are our own only if we are independent from God. Even then, we have to remember that He has made us and we have not made ourselves. Consequently, He is still Lord over us in this and all other respects, and there is not a word of our tongues for which we are not accountable to Him.

We are equally accountable to God for our hands and feet, and all the members of our body. As stewards, we cannot render them as instruments of unrighteousness. It is the purpose of God that we use them for instruments of righteousness for Him.

The same can be said for our worldly goods. God has entrusted us with food to eat, clothes to wear, and a place to live. We are stewards not only to these necessities, but also of the conveniences of life. Above all, God has committed to our charge that talent which brings about all the rest, money. This is an unspeakably great talent, if we are wise and faithful stewards of it. It is a blessing if we employ every part of it for the purposes for which our Lord has commanded us.

God has entrusted us with several talents which do not actually come under any of these headings. Included in these are bodily strength, health, a pleasing personality, an agreeable countenance, intelligence, etc. We are but stewards of the influence we have over others. That influence may come from their love and esteem of us or from our authority over them. In this life, each has power over others to do them either good or harm, or to help or hinder them in the circumstances of life. Added to these is that invaluable talent of time with which God entrusts us from moment to moment. Lastly is that talent upon which all the rest depend, and without which they would be curses rather than blessings. This is the grace of God—the power of His Holy Spirit that alone works in us all that is acceptable in His sight. We are but stewards of this grace and of the Holy Spirit. These are but loaned to us by God, and may be withdrawn from us according to His will and purpose.

In all these respects, men are but stewards of the Lord. As possessor of heaven and earth, He has committed to our charge a large portion of His goods. But man is not a steward forever. Man is not a steward for any considerable length of time. We have this trust imposed in us only during the short, uncertain space we inhabit this earth. These gifts can be used by us only so long as we remain on earth. The hour is swiftly approaching, and almost at hand, when we can no longer be stewards. The moment our spirit returns to God at death, we cease to be stewards. Then our stewardship is at its end. Part of those goods with which we were entrusted are now at an end. At least with regard to use, men are no longer entrusted with them. The parts which remain with us after we leave this life, can no longer be used or improved as they were before.

After this life we have nothing more to do with food,

clothing, housing, and other earthly possessions. All of these worldly goods are delivered into other hands. Our stewardship over them has ended. The same is true with regard to our stewardship over the body. The moment the spirit returns to God, we are no longer stewards of the body. All of the parts and members of which it was composed return to the dust. They no longer have power to move. The feet have forgotten their purpose. The flesh, sinews, and bones hasten to be dissolved back into the dust.

Then our talents of a mixed nature also end. Our strength, our health, our eloquence, our address, our faculty of pleasing, or persuading, or convincing others, will cease. Likewise, all of the honors we once enjoyed will come to an end. All of the power which was lodged in our hands will cease. All of the influence we once had over others, either by the love or the esteem they had for us, will end. Love, hatred, and all of our desires will perish. No one will care how we once thought about them. The living look upon the dead as neither being able to help or to hurt them. From this understanding comes the saying, "A living dog is better than a dead lion."[2]

Some questions may come up concerning some of the other talents with which we are now entrusted. There is no doubt that the kind of speech we now use, with our bodily organs, will be entirely at an end. It is certain that the tongue will no longer give speech and the ear will no longer hear it. Speech as we know it will cease. However, there will remain some type of communication.

It is probable that senses of the lower kind will also cease. Feeling, smell, and taste are chiefly, if not wholly, intended for the preservation of the body. But will not some kind of senses remain after death? As there will be communication, there will also be sight. There will be something in the soul equivalent to the present sense of hearing and experiencing.

It is also probable these senses will also exist in a far greater degree than now. We have a foretaste of these future experiences of the soul in this life through dreams. Seeing, hearing, experiencing, and feeling can be enjoyed by the soul in dreams while the body is disengaged from use. We are certain this occurs. We are also certain this will occur in the world to come. We are equally certain, however, our senses as we now know them are entrusted to us but for a limited time. We are only stewards of them in this life until the body is placed in the grave.

After death comes, our opportunity to gain education will cease. What knowledge or wisdom we have gained will be of no use. There will be no device whereby we may improve these talents with which we were once entrusted. At death, time is no more. The time of our trial and qualifications for everlasting happiness or misery is past. Our day, the day of man, is then over. The day of salvation is ended. Nothing remains but the day of the Lord, ushering in the wide and unchanging eternity.

Our souls, being immortal, will retain all of their faculties when our bodies are returned to the earth. Our memory, our understanding, will not be destroyed or impaired by the dissolution of the body. On the contrary, we have reason to believe they will be strengthened considerably. We have reason to believe that the limitations of the soul result from its union with the corruptible body. It is probable, at the time of separation of body and soul, our memory will recover all of its experiences. At that time, it will faithfully show everything it ever knew. Many things are frequently forgotten by men but not by spirits. From the time the soul puts off its earthly tabernacle, we believe it will forget nothing.

At that time, the understanding will be freed from defects which are now inseparable from it. From the beginning of time, it has been known that ignorance and mistake are inseparable from human nature. This assertion is only true with regard to living men and no longer applies after the soul leaves the body. Ignorance belongs to every finite understanding. There is none but God who knows all things. But when the body is laid aside, ignorance is also laid aside forever.

As the soul will retain its understanding and memory, the will also will retain its full vigor. When spirits separate themselves from bodies, they retain the capacity for love, and hope, and desire. It is probable these qualities work with a greater force than when the soul was coupled with the fallible body.

Even though these remain after death, we are no longer stewards of them. The grace which was entrusted to enable us to be faithful and wise stewards is no longer entrusted for that purpose. Being no longer stewards, we will be required to give an account of our stewardship. At our appointed time, God will inquire of us, "How did you employ your soul? I entrusted you with an immortal spirit, endowed with many faculties and powers. You were given understanding, imagination, memory, will, and emotions. I gave you full and express directions as to how all these were to be employed.

"Did you employ your understanding as far as it was capable, according to my directions? Did you employ this understanding in the knowledge of yourself and of me? Did you attempt to understand my nature, my attributes, my works, whether of creation, of providence, or of grace? Did you employ it in acquainting yourself with the Bible? Did you use every means of increasing your knowledge of my Word? Did you meditate upon it day and night?

"Did you employ your memory according to my will? Did you acquire knowledge for the good of my glory, your own salvation, and the good of others? Or did you store in your memory things of no value? Did you put in your memory the instruction you had learned from my Word and the experience you had gained from my wisdom, truth, power, and mercy?

"Did you use your imagination for painting vain images and nourishing foolish and harmful desires? Or did you use your imagination in representing to you what would profit your soul and awaken it to the truth of wisdom and holiness?

"Did you follow my directions with regard to your will? Was your will wholly given up to me? Was your will swallowed up in mine so as to never oppose my will, but always run parallel with it?

"Were your emotions placed and regulated in such a manner as I directed in my Word? Did you give me your whole heart? Did you love me rather than the world and the things of the world? Was I the sole object of your love? Was all of your desire for me in the remembrance of my name? Was I the joy of your heart, the delight of your soul, the chief among ten thousand?

"Did you sorrow for nothing but that which grieved my Spirit? Did you fear and hate nothing but sin? Did the whole stream of your affections flow back to the source from whence they came? Were your thoughts employed according to my will, not ranging to and fro to the ends of the earth? Did you keep your thoughts away from all folly and sin and upon that which is pure and holy? Did you think about those things which were conducive to my glory and which would bring about peace and good will among men?"

Then God will also ask, "How did you use the body with which I entrusted you? I gave you a tongue for praise. Did you use it to the end to which it was given? Did you employ it not in evil speaking or idle speaking, not in uncharitable or unprofitable conversation, but for good? Did you use it always to minister grace to the hearer, speaking only that which was useful to yourself or others toward that end? I gave you, together with your other senses, those great faculties of knowledge, sight, and hearing. Were they used for the great purposes for which they were given to you? Were they used for bringing you more instruction in righteousness and true holiness? I gave you hands and feet and various bodily members with which to perform the works which were prepared for you. Did you employ your body, not in doing the will of the flesh and its evil nature, or the will of the mind to which reason or fancy led you, but in the doing of my will? I sent you into the world to do my will, to work out your own salvation. Did you present all of your bodily members, not to sin as instruments of unrighteousness, but to me alone through Jesus as the instrument of righteousness?"

God will next ask, "How did you employ the worldly goods which I lodged in your hands? Did you use your food, not for happiness, but simply to preserve your body in health, strength, and vigor, as a fit instrument for your soul? Did you use your apparel, not to nourish vanity or pride, or to tempt others to sin, but to conveniently and decently defend yourself from the weather and exposure? Did you prepare and use your house, and all other conveniences, with a single eye to my glory and my purpose? In every point in your life, did you use these things not seeking your own honor but mine? Did you always plan to please me and not yourself?

"And in what manner did you employ that great talent, money? Did you use it to gratify the desire of the flesh, the desire of the eye, or the pride of life? Squandering money in vain excesses is the same as throwing it into the sea. Hoarding it up to leave it behind you is the same as burying it in the earth. Did you apply proper stewardship by first supplying your own reasonable needs, along with those of your family, then restoring the remainder to me through the poor who needed to receive it? Did you look upon yourself as only one of the poor whose wants were to be supplied from the whole which I put into your hands for that purpose? I gave you the right of being supplied first, and the blessedness of giving rather than receiving. Accordingly, were you a benefactor to all mankind? Did you feed the hungry, clothe the naked, comfort the sick, assist the stranger, and relieve the afflicted according to their various needs? Were you eyes to the blind, and feet to the lame, a father to the fatherless, and a husband to the widow? And did you labor to improve all outward works of mercy as means of saving souls from works of death?"

Then God will further inquire, "Have you been a wise and faithful steward with regard to the talents of a mixed nature which I lent to you? Did you employ your health and strength, not in folly or sin or in the pleasures which perish in using, but in a vigorous pursuit of what I charged you to do? Did you use whatever is pleasing in your personality and the advantages of your education, for the promotion of virtue in the world? Did you use those things for the enlargement of my kingdom? Did you employ your share of power and influence for the increase of wisdom and holiness of others? Did you employ your talent of time with care, duly weighing the value of every moment while knowing that all were numbered in eternity?

"Above all, were you a good steward of my grace which accompanied and followed you? Did you duly observe, and seek to improve, all of the influences of my Holy Spirit? Did you accept every desire, every measure of light, and all of the sharp and gentle reproofs of my Spirit? How did you profit by the spirit of bondage and fear which I gave you prior to the spirit of adoption? And when you were made a partaker of this Holy Spirit, and could cry in your heart, 'Abba, Father,' did you stand steadfast in that liberty? Did you, from that moment forward, present your soul and body, your thoughts, your words and actions, as one holy sacrifice? Did you then glorify me in your body and in love with your spirit? If so, you have done well and good and you are a faithful steward. You may enter into the eternal joys."

From all of these considerations, we may well learn how important is this short, uncertain moment of life. How precious, above all understanding and all conception, is every portion of life. How greatly does it concern everyone of us to let none of these moments be wasted. How important it is to improve each of them for the noblest purposes as long as we have a breath of life in us.

Next we learn there is no use of our time, no action or conversation, which is merely indifferent. All is either good or bad, because all our time, as everything we have, is not our own. All of these talents are the property of another. They are the property of God, our creator. Now, these are either employed according to His will, or they are not. If they are so employed, all is good. If they are not employed according to His will, all is evil. It is His will that we should continually grow in grace and in the living knowledge of Jesus Christ. Consequently, every thought, word, and work must be dedicated to this purpose. When the knowledge of our Lord and savior, Jesus Christ, is increased, we grow in grace. This, then, is good. Every thought, word, or work, which does not increase this knowledge, is truly and properly evil.

We learn also from this that there are no works of supererogation. We can never do more than our duty. All that we can do for God is already due to Him. This is because all that we have is not our own, but God's. We have not received only this or that from Him. We have received everything we have from Him. Therefore, everything is His due. He who gives us all, necessarily has a right to all. If we pay Him anything less than all, we are not faithful stewards.

Every man shall receive his own reward according to his own labor. This being the case, we cannot be wise stewards unless we labor to the uttermost of our power. We should not leave anything undone which we can possibly do. As stewards we must put forth all of our strength.

If anyone is to call himself a good steward of the manifold gifts of God, let him see that all of his thoughts, words, and works are agreeable to the post which God has assigned. It is no small thing to lay out for God all we have received from Him. It requires the full infilling of the Holy Spirit and all the gifts and power from His gifts and Spirit. It requires all wisdom, all resolution, all patience, and all constancy. Good stewardship requires a dedication far beyond that which one can have by nature. However, it does not require more than one may have by grace through the Holy Spirit. God's grace is sufficient for us. All things are possible to those who believe. By a living faith through the Holy Spirit, we put on the Lord Jesus Christ. We put on the whole armor of God and are enabled to glorify Him in all of our words and works. We are then able to bring every thought into captivity and into obedience to God. Total dedication to the will and purpose of God becomes our meat and drink. By grace we have received a faith which makes this dedication possible. We have received a complete new nature, being born of God and filled with the empowering Holy Spirit.

From "The Good Steward," *Forty-Four Sermons*, Sermon LI.

11

Perfection

*Not as though I had already attained, either were already
perfect. (Phil. 3:12, KJV)*

There is scarcely any expression in the Bible which has
caused more dispute than this. The word "perfect" is what
disturbs many people. The very sound is irritating.
Whoever preaches perfection, by claiming that it is
attainable in this life, runs the risk of being accounted as
worse than a heathen or a publican.

As a result, some have advised us to stop using these
expressions. But are they not found in the Word of God? If
so, by what authority can any servant of God lay them aside,
even though all men might be offended? We have not learned
such a practice from Jesus. To stop using these expressions
would be yielding to the devil. Whatever God has spoken,
that we will speak. We must speak God's Word whether men
will listen or not. A minister must speak the whole Word of
Christ. Only when he does this can he be clear of his
responsibility for other men's souls. He must not shun
proclaiming the whole counsel of God. It is Jesus himself who

149

taught, "Be ye therefore perfect, even as your Father which is in heaven is perfect."[1]

We cannot lay these expressions aside, because they are the words of God, and not men. Therefore, it is important to explain their meaning, so that the sincere Christian can remain on the straight path of God's high calling. This understanding is even more necessary because of seemingly contradictory statements by Paul. On one hand, Paul wrote, "Not as though I had already attained, either were already perfect." But several verses later, he spoke of himself and many others as perfect. There he wrote, "Let us, therefore, as many as be perfect, be thus minded."[2] To prevent any confusion, we need to know in what sense Christians are and are not perfect.

First, let us consider in what sense Christians are not perfect. From both experience and Scripture, it appears that they are not perfect in knowledge. They are not so perfect in this life as to be free from ignorance. They know, as do non-Christians, many things relating to the world. They also know the general truths which God has revealed relating to the world yet to come, those matters which are spiritually discerned, the kind of love with which God has loved them, what it is to be called the sons of God, the mighty working of the Holy Spirit in their hearts, and the wisdom of God's providence directing their paths. They believe that all things work together for their good through that providence. In every circumstance of life, they know that God requires them to act in a Christian manner. They recognize that they are required to keep their conscience free from any offense toward either God or man.

But regarding God himself, there are innumerable things they do not know. They cannot understand God perfectly—how there are three persons in one—the Father, the Son, and the Holy Spirit. They do not know how the Son of God took upon himself the form of a servant. They cannot explain any one attribute nor any one circumstance of the divine nature. They do not know the times and seasons when God will work His great works upon earth. Much less do they know when God will bring this world to an end.

Christians are required to live here in this life with this imperfect knowledge. They accept God's dealings in their lives knowing that what they do not know now, they shall know in the hereafter. And how little do they know of what is ever before them. They even lack full understanding of the visible works of God's hands. Who can explain how God hangs the earth upon nothing? Who understands how He unites all parts of His vast creation by a secret type of chain which cannot be broken? Even in the best of men, there is vast ignorance and little knowledge.

In this life, then, no one is free from ignorance. Neither is any man free from mistakes. Indeed, mistakes are an almost unavoidable consequence of ignorance. Those who only know in part are always apt to err in things because of their partial understanding.

Christians do not make mistakes in regard to the essential matters of salvation. They do not confuse spiritual darkness for light. They do not court eternal death through spiritual error. Christians have been taught of God in these matters. The way of holiness which He teaches them is plain. So it is only in things nonessential to salvation that they can make mistakes. Those errors may be frequently made. The best and wisest of men are frequently mistaken even in regard to facts. Often they believe that those things which are, are not. Conversely, they often believe that things have been done which were not. Even if they do not make mistakes as to fact itself, they may be confused regarding the circumstances of that fact. Quite often the best intentioned can believe the circumstances to be different than what, in truth, they really are. Therefore, additional mistakes result from mistaken understanding.

Christians may even be mistaken in their moral judgments. They may believe either past or present actions which were, or are evil, to be good, and such actions as were or are good, to be evil. They also may judge incorrectly with regard to the nature of men. They can conceivably suppose good men to be better, or wicked men to be worse than they really are. It is possible that a Christian may confuse a good man for a wicked man, or a wicked man for a good man.

Even with regard to the Bible itself, the best of men are liable to err. Indeed, all make mistakes daily in interpreting the Bible. This is especially true with respect to those parts of it which do not immediately relate to daily practice. Even these children of God cannot agree on the interpretation of the Bible in many places. This difference of opinion is not any proof that they are not the children of God. It is proof, however, that we are no more to expect any living man to be infallible than to be omniscient.

Some believe they know all things. To support this belief, they refer to the writings of John. He wrote, "But ye have an unction from the Holy One, and ye know all things."[3] The answer to this claim is plain. John was saying Christians know all the things that are necessary for their salvation. John never planned to extend this point. He did not speak in an absolute sense of all knowledge. This is clear, because he would set himself above Jesus if he claimed to know more. Jesus himself, as man, did not know all things. On one occasion, Jesus said, "Of that day and hour no one knows, not even the angels of heaven, nor the Son, but the Father only."[4]

John also noted in another Scripture that Christians are not without error. He stated, "I write this to you about those who would deceive you."[5] The possibility of error is also seen from his frequently repeated caution, "Let no one deceive you."[6] Such a warning would have been altogether unnecessary if Christians were not capable of making mistakes. Christians, therefore, are not so perfect as to be free from either ignorance or mistakes.

Furthermore, Christians are not free from weaknesses and infirmities. By infirmity, we mean both bodily weaknesses and inward or outward imperfections which are not of a moral nature. Included in these infirmities are the slowness of understanding. Below normal intelligence, incoherency of thought, the lack of memory, irregular imaginations, slowness of speech, impropriety of language, and pronunciation problems are included. There are, in fact, innumerable defects of both conversation and behavior. These infirmities are found in the best of men in greater or lesser degrees. It seems as if none can hope to be perfectly freed from some of these infirmities. Certainly, Christians cannot claim to be so perfect as to be totally freed from all infirmities.

Christians are not free from temptation. Such perfection does not belong to this life. It is true that some seem to be without temptation. Often this is because they have ceased to resist temptations and hardly perceive them. It is also true that many are not tempted to gross forms of sin. Satan, in his evil wisdom, has perceived them to be fast asleep in dead forms of godliness. He does not tempt them to gross sin, lest they should awake from their dead, faithless state.

There are a few Christians whom God has released from temptation for a while. For a season, it may be weeks or months, God allows them to remain on a spiritual high, free from Satan's temptations. However, we learn from the Scriptures that this state will not last forever. Jesus himself, in the days of His manhood, was tempted even to the end of His earthly life. Therefore, as the Master was, so shall the servant be.

Christian perfection, therefore, does not imply an exemption from either ignorance, mistake, infirmities, or temptations. Christian perfection is only another term for holiness. They are two names for the same thing. According to the Scripture, everyone that is holy is perfect. However, it must be observed that there is no absolute perfection on earth. There is always the necessity of perfection in degrees. There is no perfection which does not admit the need of a continual increase. No matter how much a man has attained, or in what high degree he is perfect, he still needs to grow in grace. He needs a daily advancement in the knowledge and love of God, his Savior.

Now it is important to observe in what sense a Christian is perfect. It must be observed that there are several stages in Christian life and growth. Some Christians are as newborn babes, while others are as mature adults. John himself in his first epistle uses the terms "little children," "young men," and "fathers." He says, "I am writing to you, little children, because your sins are forgiven for his sake. I am writing to you, fathers, because you know him who is from the beginning. I am writing to you, young men, because you have overcome the evil one. I write to you, children, because you know the Father. I write to you, fathers, because you know him who is from the beginning. I write to you, young men, because you are strong, and the word of God abides in you, and you have overcome the evil one."[7] Those Christians had known the Father, the Son, and the Holy Spirit in their inmost souls. They were perfect men growing up to the fullness of Christ.

They who are perfect in Christ are the only perfect Christians. It is of them that I primarily speak. But even babes in Christ are in such a sense perfect, born of God, so as not to commit sin. If there is any doubt of this privilege of

Christians, the question need not be decided by abstract reasonings. Such debate is only drawn out into needless length, and always leaves the point undecided. Neither is it necessary to determine this point by the experience of any particular person. Many believe that they do not commit sin when they actually do. However, this proves nothing either way. We can appeal the question to the law and the testimony of the Bible. We abide by God's Word alone. By that Word we are to be judged.

The Word of God plainly declares that those who are justified, who are born again in the lowest sense, do not commit sin.[8] Christians do not live any longer in sin. Their old man is crucified in Christ, and they are planted together in His likeness through His death. The body of sin is destroyed so that they do not serve sin. Being dead with Christ, they are free from sin.[9] They are dead to sin and alive to God. Sin has no more dominion over them. They are no longer under the law, but are now under grace. So it is that these being free from sin have become servants of righteousness.[10]

The very least which can be implied from these words is that all real Christians, or believers in Christ, are made free from outward sin. And the same freedom which Paul expresses here is also claimed by Peter. He wrote, "Since therefore Christ suffered in the flesh, arm yourselves with the same thought, for whoever has suffered in the flesh has ceased from sin, so as to live for the rest of the time in the flesh no longer by human passions, but by the will of God."[11] This ceasing from sin, interpreted in the lowest sense, regards only the outward behavior. It denotes the ceasing from the outward act, from any outward transgression of the law.

The clearest words of all come from John in the third chapter of his first letter. "He who commits sin is of the devil, for the devil has sinned from the beginning. The reason the Son of God appeared was to destroy the works of the devil. No one born of God commits sin, for God's nature abides in him, and he cannot sin because he is born of God."[12] And later in the same letter he wrote, "We know that any one born of God does not sin, but He who was born of God keeps him, and the evil one does not touch him."[13]

Some would like to add a condition to this statement. They would alter the teaching to say that a Christian does not sin habitually or willfully. They would teach that the Christian does not sin as other men do. They would say that he does not sin as much as he did before. Such conditions are not found in the Bible. John is firm and absolute. Any dilution of his statement must be denied unless it can be proved from the Word of God.

Peter testifies that this great salvation from sin came after Jesus was glorified. He spoke of his brothers in the flesh now having received the end of their faith, the salvation of their souls. He wrote, "As the outcome of your faith you obtain the salvation of your souls. The prophets who prophesied of the grace that was to be yours searched and inquired about this salvation."[14] This is the gracious dispensation that was to come through Christ. The sufferings of Christ and His subsequent glory were predicted and revealed before they occurred. Also predicted was this glorious salvation from sins that would follow. "It was revealed to them that they were serving not themselves but you, in the things which have now been announced to you by those who preached the good news to you through the Holy Spirit sent from heaven, things into which angels long to look."[15] This occurred on the day of Pentecost. That Pentecostal event of the Holy Spirit continues to occur throughout all generations in the hearts of all true believers. It is on this foundation of grace imparted to all true believers by the revelation of Jesus Christ that all may be assured of the promises and remain free from sin.

Still, there are those who would attempt to prove that the apostle's words, "He that is born of God sins not," are not to be understood according to this obvious meaning. For proof, they would say the apostles themselves committed sin. They would point to Peter and Paul to prove the point. Paul would be cited for his sharp contention with Barnabas, and Peter for his hypocrisy at Antioch. Because two of the apostles did once sin, they would imply that all Christians of all ages will commit sin as long as they live.

It is childish reasoning to state that all must sin because one did. There is no necessity of sinning simply because some do. The grace of God is sufficient for us at all times. When temptation to sin comes, there is a way to escape it. Those who are tempted to sin need not yield. No man is tempted above what he is able to bear. In no way do the experiences of the apostles clash with John's assertion, "He who is born of God does not sin."

Some will accuse John of contradicting himself. In one place he says, "Whoever is born of God does not commit sin." Yet in another place he says, "If we say we have no sin, we deceive ourselves, and the truth is not in us."[16] Still again he wrote, "If we say we have not sinned, we make him a liar, and his word is not in us."[17] Understanding John's meaning is not difficult if we observe that the tenth verse fixes the sense of the eighth verse. First he says, "If we say we have no sin," and then next he says, "If we say we have not sinned." Both verses are conditioned by the ninth verse which is, "If we confess our sins, he is faithful and just, and will forgive our sins and cleanse us from all unrighteousness." It is as if John has said, "I have already affirmed that the blood of Jesus cleanses us from all sin." Let no man say, "I do not need this cleansing for I have no sin to be cleansed from." If we say that we have no sin, that we have not sinned, we deceive ourselves and make God a liar. If we confess our sins he is faithful and just in forgiving our sins and cleansing us from all unrighteousness. When that occurs, we may go and sin no more.

In this, John is consistent with himself and all of the other holy writers. This is even more clear when we place all of his writings concerning this in one view. First he declares, "The blood of Jesus Christ cleanses us from all sin." Secondly, no man can say that he has not sinned or that he has no sin which needs cleansing. Third, God is ready to forgive all past sins and also to save us from them for the time to come. Fourth, John has written these things so that none need to sin. But, if any man should sin, or has sinned, he doesn't need to continue in sin. He is freed from this condition through his advocate with the Father—Jesus Christ, the righteous. So his meaning is clear.

John resumed this same subject in his third chapter to remove any remaining doubt. There he explains his own meaning, "Little children, let no one deceive you. He who does right is righteous, as he is righteous. He who commits sin is of the devil; for the devil has sinned from the beginning. By this it may be seen who are the children of God, and who are the children of the devil; whoever does not do right is not of God, nor he who does not love his brother."[18] Here is the last doubt settled in the clearest manner. The doctrine of John, and the whole tenor of the New Testament, is to state that a Christian does not commit sin. In that he does not commit sin, he is perfect.

This is the privilege of every Christian even though he is but a babe in Christ. The more mature Christians are perfect in a second sense. They are free from evil thoughts and evil emotions. To clarify this, it must be first observed that thoughts concerning evil are not always evil thoughts. A thought concerning sin and a sinful thought are different. One may think of a murder which has been committed. This is no evil or sinful thought even though the thought concerns a sin. Jesus himself thought of and understood evil things. Yet Jesus had no evil or sinful thought, nor was He capable of having any. It follows that neither have any real Christians such thoughts. Every one of them who is perfect is as was Jesus.[19] Therefore, if Jesus were free from evil or sinful thoughts, so, also, Christians.

Indeed, how can evil thoughts proceed out of the heart of one who is in Jesus? If a man's heart is no longer evil, evil thoughts cannot proceed out of it. Paul affirms this privilege of all real Christians. He asserted from his own experience, "The weapons of our warfare are not carnal, but mighty through God to the pulling down of strongholds," and "casting down imaginations and every high thing that exalteth itself against the knowledge of God, and bringing into captivity every thought to the obedience of Christ."[20] So it is that Christians indeed are freed from evil thoughts.

By the same means, Christians are freed from evil tempers. This is evident from the declaration of Jesus, "A disciple is not above his teacher, nor a servant above his master; it is enough for the disciple to be like his teacher, and the servant like his master."[21] Because Jesus was free from all sinful tempers, His disciples are also. Thus, every real Christian is perfect in this sense. This is affirmed by St. Paul, who said, "I am crucified with Christ; nevertheless I live; yet not I, but Christ liveth in me."[22] These words manifestly describe a deliverance from inward as well as outward sin. This is expressed both negatively, "I live not"—my evil nature, the body of sin, is destroyed; and positively, "Christ lives in me." Therefore, all that is holy, just, and good lives in the real Christian. Both of these expressions, "Christ lives in me," and "I live not," are inseparably connected. There can be no communion between good and evil. To be in Christ is to be out of sin.

The Holy Spirit who lives in the true believer purifies his heart by faith. Everyone who has Christ in him, the hope of glory, purifies himself, even as Jesus is pure.[23] The Christian is purified from pride, because Jesus was lowly of heart. He is pure from self-will or desire, because Jesus desired only to do the will of God, and to finish His work. The Christian is pure from anger, in the common sense of the word. This is because Jesus was meek and gentle, patient, and long-suffering. We say in the common sense of the word, because all anger is not evil. Jesus himself once looked around in anger.[24] The next word, *sullupeomia*, showed that He was simultaneously grieved for the hardness of their hearts. So while He was angry at the sin, He was in the same moment grieved for the sinners. He was angry and displeased at the offense, but sorry for the offenders. He looked upon the offenders with grief and love. We who are perfect will do likewise. We can thus be angry and yet not sin. We can feel displeasure at every offense against God while loving the offender.

In this way Jesus does save His people from sin. He saves them not only from outward sin but from the inward sins of the heart. He saves them from evil thoughts and from evil tempers. So John could write, "Herein is our love made perfect, that we may have boldness in the day of judgment: because as he is, so are we in this world."[25] Beyond all contradiction, here John speaks of himself and other living Christians. He flatly affirms that not only at or after death, but in this world, they are all as their Master, Jesus.

This is a continuation of his thought which was expressed in the first part of his letter. There he wrote, "God is light, and in him is no darkness at all. If we walk in the light, as he is in the light, we have fellowship with one another, and the blood of Jesus, his Son, cleanses us from all sin."[26] "If we confess our sins, he is faithful and just, and will forgive our sins and cleanse us from all unrighteousness."[27] It is evident from this that John is speaking of a deliverance brought about in this world. He does not say that the blood of Jesus will cleanse us at the hour of death or at the day of judgment. It cleanses us at the present time. It cleanses all living Christians from all sin.

It is equally evident that if any sin remains, we are not cleansed from all sin. If any unrighteousness remains in the soul, it is not cleansed from all unrighteousness. Never let any sinner justify his continual sinning by confusing this promise. The promise is that Jesus first forgives our sins and next cleanses us from all unrighteousness. So it is that all Christians are saved in this world from all sin and from all unrighteousness. Now they are in such a sense as to be perfect, as not to commit sin, and to be freed from evil thoughts and evil tempers.

Here it is that God has fulfilled the things He spoke to us by His prophets. These promises were made since the world began, by Moses in particular, who said, "The Lord your God will circumcise your heart and the heart of your offspring, so that you will love the Lord your God with all your heart and with all your soul."[28] This promise was remarkably clear in the words of Ezekiel who spoke, "I will sprinkle clean water upon you, and you shall be clean from all your uncleannesses, and from all your idols I will cleanse you. A new heart I will give you, and a new spirit I will put within you . . . and cause you to walk in my statutes and be careful to observe my ordinances. You shall be my people, and I will be your God. I will deliver you from all your uncleannesses . . . Thus says the Lord God: On the day that I cleanse you from all your iniquities . . . the nations that are left round about you shall know that I the Lord have rebuilt the ruined places . . . I, the Lord, have spoken it, and I will do it."[29]

These promises of both the law and the prophets have been fulfilled and confirmed to us in the gospel by Jesus and His apostles. The new spirit, the Holy Spirit, was made available upon the day of Pentecost. Through God's Spirit we may be cleansed from all filthiness of flesh and spirit, being perfected in holiness in the fear of God. It is important now to forget those things which are behind and reach forth to those things which are in front. All may press forward toward the mark for the prize of the high calling of God available in Jesus Christ. Serious Christians cry unto Jesus day and night until they are delivered from the bondage of corruption into the glorious liberty of perfection as sons of God.

From "Christian Perfection," *Forty-Four Sermons*, Sermon XXXV.

12

The Holy Spirit in God's Plan

And they were all filled with the Holy Spirit. (Acts 4:31)

This same expression also appears in the second chapter of Acts where we read, "When the day of Pentecost was fully come, they were all with one accord in one place. And suddenly there came a sound from heaven as of a rushing, mighty wind, and it filled all the house where they were sitting. And there appeared unto them cloven tongues like as of fire, and it sat upon each of them. And they were all filled with the Holy Ghost."[1]

One immediate effect of this was that they began to speak with other tongues. Parthians, Medes, Elamites, and other strangers who had gathered around heard the disciples speak in their own tongues through this wonderful work of God.

Acts 4:31 informs us that when the apostles and the brethren had been praying and praising God, the place was shaken where they were meeting. Then they were all filled with the Holy Spirit. There was no visible appearance of the Holy Spirit in this instance. Neither were the extraordinary

163

gifts of healing, the working of miracles, prophecy, discerning of spirits, the speaking of various kinds of tongues, and the interpretation of tongues given here by the Holy Spirit as in other times. Each of these extraordinary gifts of the Holy Spirit was discussed in chapter 7. It is not necessary to review them at this point. However, it is necessary to observe that even in the infancy of the church, God divided these gifts with a sparing hand. Even then, not all were prophets. Not all were workers of miracles. Not all had the gift of healing. Not all spoke in tongues. In no way did all have all of the extraordinary gifts of the Holy Spirit. Perhaps none but the teachers of the church had those gifts.[2] It was, therefore, for a more important purpose that all were filled with the Holy Spirit.

The Holy Spirit was to give them what is essential for all Christians in all ages. It was to give them the mind which was in Jesus. It was to give them the holy fruit of the Spirit, without which no one is a Christian. The Holy Spirit was to fill them with love, joy, peace, long-suffering, gentleness, and goodness.[3] The Holy Spirit would endue them with faith, fidelity, meekness, and temperance. God's Spirit would enable them to crucify the flesh with its affections and lusts, its passions and desires. As a result of that inward change, they would be able to fulfill all outward righteousness. Through the work of the Holy Spirit, Christians could walk as Jesus also walked in the work of faith, in the patience of hope, and in the labor of love.[4]

Without returning to the debate concerning the extraordinary gifts of the Spirit, we can take a closer look at these ordinary fruits of the Spirit. These fruits are assured to all who are baptized with the Holy Spirit. They are to remain in the church throughout all ages. It is this great work of God in the lives of men which can be expressed by one word, true Christianity. Such Christianity does not simply imply a fixed set of opinions or a system of doctrines. True Christianity refers to men's hearts and lives. This consideration of true Christianity is divided into three areas. They are Christianity as beginning to exist in individuals, as spreading from one to another, and finally as covering the earth.

The Holy Spirit in God's plan begins with its first existence in individuals. Many of those who heard the Apostle Peter preaching repentance from sins were convicted of sin, repented, and believed in Jesus. This belief, or faith in Jesus, was an operation of God. It was the very substance of things hoped for.[5] A demonstrative evidence of these spiritual things was that one instantly received God's spirit of adoption. From that moment, the individual's prayers would be to God whom he came to know as father—"Abba, Father."[6] From this faith, he could for the first time call Jesus, "Lord," through the inspiration of the Holy Spirit.[7] The Holy Spirit himself bore witness with the Christian's spirit that he was now a child of God.[8] For the first time he could truly say, "It is no longer I who live, but Christ who lives in me; and the life I now live in the flesh I live by faith in the Son of God, who loved me and gave himself for me."[9]

This was the very essence of Christian faith. It was a divine conviction of the love of God the Father through Jesus, His Son. Through it, a sinner was now accepted into the family. Now, experiencing justification and salvation by this faith, he had peace with God.[10] This peace which passes all understanding was the peace of God ruling in his heart. It was an experience far beyond mere rational understanding. It kept the Christian's heart and mind from all doubt and fear, through the knowledge of Jesus in whom he now believed. He stood fast believing in Jesus, unafraid of any evil things. He did not fear what man could do to him, because he knew the very hairs on his head were numbered. He did not fear the powers of Satan, knowing that God had once and for all overcome that evil one. He was no longer afraid to die. Conversely, he desired to depart and be with Jesus.[11] He was assured that Jesus, through death, had destroyed Satan, who had the power of death. The result was that he was delivered from a lifetime of bondage to the fear of death.[12]

He had joy unspeakable. He rejoiced in Jesus who had reconciled him to God, his Father. His soul magnified the Lord, and his spirit rejoiced in Jesus, his Savior, in whom he had redemption in His blood and forgiveness from his sins. He rejoiced in the witness of God's Holy Spirit with his spirit that he was a child of God. The Christian rejoiced even more in the hope of attaining the glorious image of God. He sought a full renewal of his soul in righteousness and true holiness. This was to be his glory, an incorruptible inheritance which was undefiled and would not fade away.

The love of God filled his heart by the Holy Spirit who was given to him.[13] He was now a son of God, because he had been given the Holy Spirit through Jesus. Now he could cry out, "Abba, Father."[14] This parental love of God was continually increased by the witness that he had within himself.[15] God was the desire of his eyes and the joy of his heart.

The man who loved God in this manner could not help loving his brother, also. He loved his brother not only in word, but in deed and in truth. He testified, "If God so loved us, we also ought to love one another."[16] He loved every man because the mercy of God extends over all of His creatures.[17] There were no exceptions to this widespread love of mankind. A Christian could love even those whom he had never seen. He loved those of whom he knew nothing simply because they were the offspring of God. He knew Jesus had died for their souls, also. His love of others did not exclude the evil or unthankful. It even encompassed his own enemies, those who hated, persecuted, or despitefully used him. He made a place in his heart and prayed for all these people. He loved all others even as Christ loved us.

God's love taught every soul in which it dwelled humility, because love is not puffed up.[18] The result: the Christian became lowly of heart and little in his own eyes. He neither sought nor received the praise of men. He sought only the praise which comes from God. He was meek and long-suffering, gentle to all, and easy to be entreated. Faithfulness and truth were written on his heart. By the Holy Spirit, he was able to be tempered in all things. He was crucified to the world, and the world crucified to him. He was superior to every desire of the flesh, desire of the eye, and pride of life. By this same mighty power of the Holy Spirit, he was saved from both passion and pride. This almighty love removed lust, vanity, ambition, covetousness, and every emotion which was not in Jesus.

He who had this love in his heart could not do evil to his neighbor. It was impossible for him to knowingly do any harm to any man. He kept his distance from cruelty and wrong. He was careful of his conversation, avoiding any offensive speech either against justice, mercy, or truth. He put aside all lying, falsehood, and fraud. He spoke evil of no man. No unkind words ever came out of his mouth.

He was totally aware of that truth, "Without me you can do nothing." Consequently, he knew he had need of God's Spirit at every moment. He continued daily in all of the ordinances of God, seeking out all channels of God's grace to man. He met with congregations of believers as often as possible, receiving the communion bread and wine as frequently as he could. Through these, he grew daily in grace. He increased in strength in the knowledge and love of God.

Simply abstaining from evil did not satisfy him. He had a deep desire to do good. His heart continually spoke, "My Father works, and I work, also. Jesus went about doing good. I should follow in His steps." Therefore, as he had opportunity, he did all the good he could. He fed the hungry, clothed the naked, helped the stranger, and visited them who were sick or in prison. He gave his money to feed the poor. He rejoiced in working for and suffering with them. He sought out places where he might aid another and deny himself. He thought he had nothing too dear to give up for the needy. He always remembered the teachings of Jesus, "Inasmuch as ye have done it unto one of the least of these my brethren, ye have done it unto me."[19]

This is the way Christianity was in the beginning. This is a picture of the earliest Christians. Every one of them witnessed to their faith in this manner after they were filled with the Holy Spirit. All of them were of one heart and one soul. The love of Jesus, in whom they believed, caused them to love one another. None said that any of the things he owned was his own. They held all things in common. This is how completely they were crucified to the world and the world to them. "And all who believed were together and had all things in common; and they sold their possessions and goods and distributed them to all, as any had need."[20]

We observe that Christianity spread gradually throughout the world. This was the will of God, who did not light a candle to put it under a bushel, but to light the world. He lit the light of Christianity so it might give light to all who were in the world. Jesus gave the commandment, "Let your light so shine before men, that they may see your good works and give glory to your Father who is in heaven."[21]

Which of the early believers would have been unconcerned at the sight of the misery of the world? Which of them would be without compassion toward all the needy for whom Jesus died? Their hearts would melt for every troubled person. They could not stand idle all day long. Their love caused them to labor, by all possible means, to carry the saving message to those who were outside the faith. These Spirit-filled Christians spared no pains to bring all those they could to the shepherd, Jesus.[22] They labored at every opportunity to do good to all men, warning them to flee from the wrath to come. They preached that the times of ignorance of God were gone, that God called all men everywhere to repent. They called everyone to turn away from evil ways. They reasoned with them about temperance, righteousness, and justice. They preached about the judgment to come, of the wrath of God, which would surely be executed on evildoers in that day in which Jesus would judge the world.[23]

They sought to communicate with every man according to his needs. To the careless they preached, "Awake you that sleep, arise from the dead, and Christ shall give you life." To those who were already aware of their sin and groaning under conviction, they said, "We have an advocate with the Father; He is the propitiation for our sins." Those who believed they provoked to greater love and to more good works. They exhorted one another to abound more and more in holiness without which no man can see the Lord.[24]

Their efforts were not in vain. God's Word spread, and He was glorified. God's truth grew and prevailed. But at the same time, there were offenses against Christians and priests. The world was offended, because Christians testified that the works of it were evil.[25] Pleasure-seekers were offended, because they were reproved by the Christians. They objected because Christians claimed to have the knowledge of God and to be children of God. Christians were different from other men. They abstained from the fashionable ways and from all uncleanness. They made boasts that God was their Father. The unbelievers objected even more because many of their companions left them for the Christian faith.

Men of great reputations were angry because they lost the esteem of the people as the gospel spread. Christians no longer dared to give them flattering titles. They would not give homage to man which was due only to God. Tradesmen began to lose their livelihood which came from superstitions.[26]

Religious leaders were even more upset. Those so-called men of religion were of outside religion only. They accused the Christians of inciting rebellion throughout the world.[27] They said they were teaching men everywhere against the people, and against the law.[28]

The more Christianity spread, the more hurt was done by those who did not receive it. The number of those who were more and more enraged at the Christians increased daily. Christians were thus accused of turning the world upside down. More and more men cried out, "Away with such persons from the earth. It is not fit that they should live." They sincerely believed that whoever killed Christians would be doing God a favor. Christians everywhere were spoken against. Men said all kinds of evil about them, casting the name about as though it were evil. It was the same treatment received by the prophets that came before them. Some suffered only shame and reproach, but others suffered the ruin of their property. Some had the trial of mocking and scourging, but others were imprisoned. Still others died for the cause.[29]

The world was shaken, but the kingdom of God continued to spread. Sinners everywhere were turning from darkness to the light of the faith, and from the power of Satan to God. God gave Christians such wisdom and speech that their adversaries could not resist them. The witness of their lives was of as great a force as were their words. Above all, their sufferings spoke to all the world. They showed themselves to be servants of God in afflictions, in distress, in beatings, in imprisonments, in tumults, and in labors. They were steadfast in the dangers at sea, the dangers in the wilderness, in weariness, and in pain, and in hunger, and in thirst, and in nakedness. And when, after having lived their witness, they were led as sheep to the slaughter, they gratefully gave up their lives as a sacrifice and service of their faith. When they died, it seemed as if their lives had a voice. The heathen watched and admitted, "He, being dead, yet speaks."

But, as Christianity spread, weeds appeared with the wheat. The mystery of iniquity was at work as well as the mystery of godliness. Soon Satan found a place even in the temple of God. Because of this, many Christians became less faithful and returned to the world. The increasing corruptions of the succeeding generations of Christians is well known and has been fully described. Nonetheless, witnesses to God were raised up. They showed that Jesus had built His church on a rock and that the gates of hell should not prevail against her.[30]

Can Satan cause the truth of God to fail, or His promises to be of no effect? No! The time will come when Christianity will prevail over all. Christianity will cover the whole earth. What a strange sight this will be—a Christian world. Ancient prophets wondered about this and searched the Scriptures. The Holy Spirit which was in them testified, "It shall come to pass in the latter days that the mountain of the house of the Lord shall be established as the highest of the mountains, and shall be raised above the hills; and all the nations shall flow to it . . . and they shall beat their swords into plowshares, and their spears into pruning hooks; nation shall not lift up sword against nation, neither shall they learn war any more."[31]

"In that day the root of Jesse shall stand as an ensign to the peoples; him shall the nations seek, and his dwelling shall be glorious. In that day, the Lord will extend his hand yet a second time to recover the remnant which is left of his people. . . . He will raise an ensign for the nations, and will assemble the outcasts of Israel, and gather the dispersed of Judah from the four corners of the earth."[32] "The wolf shall dwell with the lamb, and the leopard shall lie down with the kid, and the calf and the lion and the fatling together, and a little child shall lead them. They shall not hurt nor destroy in all my holy mountain; for the earth shall be full of the knowledge of the Lord as the waters cover the sea."[33]

The words of the Apostle Paul affirm the same. It is evident they have not yet been fulfilled. He wrote, "Hath God cast away his people? God forbid: but rather through their fall salvation is come unto the Gentiles. . . . And the diminishing of them the riches of the Gentiles how much more their fulness? . . . For I would not, brethren, that ye should be ignorant of this mystery . . . blindness in part is happened to Israel, until the fulness of the Gentiles be come in. And so all Israel shall be saved."[34]

Imagine what it will be like when these prophecies shall be accomplished in the fullness of the time. What a prospect this is. All is peace, quietness, and assurance forever. There is no din of arms, no confused noise, no garments rolled in blood. Destructions have come to a perpetual end. Wars have ceased from the earth. No brother rises up against his brother. No country or city is divided against itself, tearing itself asunder. Civil discord is at an end forever. None is left to either harm or destroy his neighbor. There is no oppression to make even the wise man mad. There is no extortion to grind the face of the poor. There is no more wrong, robbery, plunder, or injustice. Now all are content with those things which they possess. Thus, righteousness and peace have kissed each other. Righteousness, flourishing out of the earth, has taken root and filled the land. Peace now looks down on earth from heaven.

With this righteousness and justice, mercy is also found. The earth is no longer full of cruel habitations. The Lord has destroyed both the bloodthirsty and the malicious. The envious and revengeful man is gone. Where there was provocation, there is none now. No one knows how to return evil for evil. There is none that does evil, not even one. All are now harmless as doves. Being filled with peace and joy in the Holy Spirit, through believing, all are united in that one body through that one Spirit. All love one another as brothers. All are of one heart and one soul. None say that any of the things which he possesses is his own. There is no one among them who has material needs. Every man loves his neighbor as himself. All walk by one rule, "Whatever you would have men do unto you, even so do that unto them."

It follows that no unkind word can ever be heard among them. There is no strife in conversation. There is no contention of any kind, no railing or evil speaking. Everyone speaks with wisdom and in his tongue is the law of kindness. Men are equally incapable of fraud or guile. Their love is not feigned. Their words are always the exact expression of their thoughts, opening a window to their heart. Whoever desires to look into his heart will see that only love and God are there.

When Jesus subdues all things to himself, He will cause every heart to overflow with love and will fill every mouth with praise. "Happy the people to whom such blessings fall! Happy the people whose God is the Lord!"[35]

So the Lord says, "Arise, shine; for your light has come, and the glory of the Lord has risen upon you."[36] "You shall know that I, the Lord, am your Savior and your Redeemer, the Mighty One of Jacob. . . . I will make your overseers peace and your taskmasters righteousness. Violence shall no more be heard in your land, devastation or destruction within your borders; you shall call your walls Salvation and your gates Praise. . . . Your people shall all be righteous; they shall possess the land forever, the shoot of my planting, the work of my hands, that I might be glorified. The sun shall be no more your light by day, nor for brightness shall the moon give light to you by night; but the Lord will be your everlasting light, and your God will be your glory."[37]

We have now considered Christianity as beginning, as going on, and as covering the whole earth. What then is the practical application of this?

Where does this Christianity exist now? Where do these Christians live? Which is the country where the inhabitants are thus filled with the Holy Spirit? Where are all of one heart and one soul in the Lord? Where are those who will not allow anyone among them to lack anything? Do they exist who continually give to every man according to his need? Do one and all have the love of God filling their hearts? Where are those who have such a love as to require them to love their neighbor as themselves? Where are those who have put on mercy, humbleness of mind, gentleness, long-suffering, and therefore offend no one by either word or deed? Are there people who in every point do to all men as they would have done unto themselves? Can we call any country a Christian country which does not answer this description? If not, we must admit there has never been a Christian country on the earth.

Look around you and answer this question for yourself. Is your city a Christian city? Is Christianity, scriptural Christianity found there? Are the citizens, as a community of men, filled with the Holy Spirit? Do they enjoy in their hearts, and show forth in their lives, the genuine fruits of that Spirit? Are all of the leaders, educators, and elected officials of one heart and one soul? Is the love of God shed abroad in their hearts? Are all of their desires and emotions the same as were in Jesus? Are all of their lives lived in conformance to Jesus' principles? Is every one of them as holy as Jesus called us to be holy in all manner of conversation?

More specifically, how does your own conscience and heart witness to you? Are you filled with the Holy Spirit? Are you an honest reflection of Jesus whom you were appointed to represent here on earth? In all of your places in this life, are you a testimony to all that the Lord is your governor? Are all the thoughts of your heart, all your emotions and desires suitable to your high calling as a Christian? Are all of the words which come out of your mouth as those that come out of the mouth of God? Is there dignity and love in all of your actions? Is there greatness in your life which flows only from a heart full of God?

And what about you who were especially called to raise and train children? Are you filled with the Holy Spirit? Do you exhibit all of the fruits of the Spirit which your position so indispensably requires? Is your heart whole with God? Are you full of love and zeal to set up God's kingdom on earth? Do you continually remind those in your care of the one end of all our endeavors—to know, love, and serve the only true God and Jesus Christ whom He has sent? Do you daily seek to cultivate in them that love which never fails? Do you teach that without the love of God, all is but splendid ignorance, pompous folly, and vexation of spirit? Does all you teach, by words and example, tend to the love of God and to all mankind for His sake? Do you keep your eye on this goal in whatever you prescribe? Is it your plan to lead each of those in your care so they may become burning and shining

lights, loving the gospel of Jesus in all things? Do you put
forth all of your strength in this great work with which you
have been entrusted? Do you labor in it with all your might?
Do you exert every faculty of your soul, with all your power,
toward this end?

I do not speak here as if you and all under your care were
to be clergymen. I speak only as if all of you were to be
Christians. What example is set by us as Christians? Do you
abound in the fruits of the Spirit? Do you reflect a lowliness
of mind in self-denial and mortification, and a seriousness
and composure of spirit? Do you show meekness, sobriety,
patience, and temperance? Is your example of unwearied
restless effort to do good of every kind to all men, to relieve
their outward needs, to bring their souls to the true
knowledge and love of God? Is this the general character of
most of us? Rather, have not pride, haughtiness,
impatience, peevishness, sloth, indolence, gluttony, and
sensuality been charged to us by our detractors, often not
wholly without grounds? Oh, that God would roll away this
criticism from us, and that the very memory of it would
perish from us.

Many of us claim to be more immediately consecrated to
God. Some publicly claim specific ministries. Are we then
examples in word, conversation, charity, spirit, faith, and
purity?[38] Is a holiness to the Lord written on our faces and
on our countenances? From what motives do we claim this
office? Was it with a single eye to serve God, trusting we
were inwardly called by the Holy Spirit to assume this task
for the promotion of His glory and the edifying of the people?
Are we clearly committed, by God's grace, to give ourselves
fully to this cause? Do we forsake and set aside all worldly
cares and studies for the benefit of our call? Do we apply
ourselves wholly to this one thing, and draw all our cares and
studies this way?

When we attempt to teach, are we ourselves taught of God that we may be able to teach others, also? Do we know the mind of God? Do we know the mind of Jesus? Has God revealed His Son in us? Has God really given us grace to be ministers of the New Covenant? Where are the seals of the apostleship? How many persons who were dead in sin and doubt have been brought to Jesus by our word? Have we such a burning zeal to save souls from death that we often forget our own needs? Do we speak plainly, avoiding confusion, to bring every man into the sight of God? Are we dead to the world, and the things of the world, laying up all our treasures in heaven? Do we lord over others our faith, or are we the least, the servants of all? When we receive the reproach of Jesus, does it depress us? Can we rejoice in that reproach? When we are hit on one cheek, do we resent it? Are we patient with those who affront us? Are we willing to turn the other cheek, also, not resisting evil, but overcoming evil with good? Have we bitter zeal, inciting us to strive sharply and passionately with those who disagree? Is our zeal aflame with love, so as to direct all our words with sweetness, lowliness, and meekness?

What shall we say to those exposed to our witness? Have we either the form or power of Christian godliness? Are we humble, teachable, or advisable? Are we stubborn, self-willed, heady, and high-minded? Are we obedient to our superiors as we are to our parents? Do we resent those to whom we owe reverence? Are we diligent in all our responsibilities, pursuing them with all our strength? Do we redeem the time, crowding as much work into every day as possible? Are we concerned with the time spent each day in reading and conversation that has no tendency toward our Christian growth?

What is our example in the matter of money management? Do we take care, out of principle, to owe no man anything?

Do we remember the sabbath and always keep it holy? Is it always spent in the direct worship of God? When we are in church, do we remember that God is there? Do we behave as though we can see Him who is invisible? Do we possess our bodies in total honor and sanctification as the temple of the Holy Spirit? Is any drunkenness and uncleanness found in us? Do any of us take the name of the Lord in vain without remorse or fear? Are there not some of us who swear? Oh, what a weight of sin lies upon most of us. God is not blind to it.

The result of this is that most of this generation are triflers. They are triflers with God, with one another, and with their own souls. How few spend, from one week to another, an uninterrupted hour of private prayer with God. How few have any thought of God in their general conversation. How few are acquainted in any degree with the work of the Holy Spirit, and His supernatural work in the souls of men. How few can bear, except now and then in a church, any talk of the Holy Spirit. When one talks of the Holy Spirit, he is usually thought of as a hypocrite or a fanatic. What kind of Christian is it who is uncomfortable with the talk of Christianity? Oh, what a Christian nation this is. It is time for God to take us all into His own hand. What probability, what possibility is there that scriptural Christianity will be the religion of the land? Is there any possibility that all men will be filled with the Holy Spirit and show it in their speech and lives? Who can bring about this genuine Christianity? Will it be by you who have received the Holy Spirit? Is your life, wealth, and liberty important enough to cause you to be an instrument in bringing this about?

If you have this desire, do you have the power to effect it? Perhaps you have made a few attempts with small success. Have some objected to your efforts saying, "You criticize us"? Can Christianity be restored by our small, inconsiderable effort? We must put ourselves to the test. Iniquity has overspread us like a flood. If not us, what then shall God send? Must He send famine, plague, or war to reform us?

Lord, save us, or we perish. Lift us out of this mire, so we do not sink. Help us against all of these enemies. As men, we are unable to help ourselves. Through you, all things are possible according to the greatness of your power. Preserve us according to your will through the power of your Holy Spirit. Bring about scriptural Christianity through the fullness of the Holy Spirit in our lives and in this world.

From "Scriptural Christianity," *Forty-Four Sermons*, Sermon IV.

13

True Christianity

There have been too many disputes, for too long, about who is Christian, and the nature of true Christianity. The points of debate have been who is a real Christian and what is genuine Christianity. What is the evidence of genuine Christianity? What is the surest and most accessible evidence by which one may know it is of God? It is important to consider each of these matters, in the hope that debate may be ended.

Who is a Christian, indeed? What does this term imply? It has been abused for so long, it appears to mean nothing. Possibly it means worse than nothing. In history, the term has been a cloak for the vilest hypocrisy and the grossest immoralities. Certainly it is time to rescue the name from the hands of those who are a reproach to human nature. It is time to show clearly what manner of man he is to whom the name Christian rightfully belongs.

A true Christian cannot think about God without being humbled. He has a deep sense of the distance between man on earth and God who sits in the heavens. In God's presence he sinks to his knees, knowing himself to be little. He is conscious, in a manner words cannot express, of his own littleness, ignorance, and foolishness. It is a true Christian who can cry out from the fullness of his heart, "Oh, God, what is man? What am I?"

A Christian has a continual sense of his dependence upon the parent of good for his being and all the blessings which attend it. To God he attributes every natural and every moral endowment which he possesses. He credits God with all that is commonly ascribed to fortune or to wisdom, courage, or merit. Therefore, he willingly complies with whatever appears to be God's will, not only with patience, but also with thankfulness. He willingly resigns all that he is, all that he has, to God's wise and gracious disposal. The ruling desire of his heart is absolute submission and tenderest gratitude to his sovereign God. This grateful love creates an awesome reverence toward God and an earnest desire not to allow any disposition, action, word, or thought, which might in any degree displease Him. He always wants to please his indulgent Father to whom he owes his life, breath, and all things.

This true Christian has the strongest love for God. Knowing God as the fountain of all good, he has a firm confidence in Him. He has a confidence which neither pleasure nor pain, life nor death, can shake. But this confidence, far from creating sloth or indolence, pushes him to the most vigorous industry. It causes him to exert all of his strength in obeying God. Therefore, he is never faint in mind, never weary of doing whatever he believes to be God's will. He knows the most acceptable worship is to imitate God and he continually labors to transcribe in himself all of God's imitable perfection. In particular he seeks to express God's justice, mercy, and truth.

Above all, remembering that God is love, the Christian is conformed to the same likeness. He is full of love for his neighbor—a universal love not confined to one sect or party. His love is not restricted to those who agree with him in opinions or modes of worship. It is not reserved for those who are related to him by blood or by marriage. Neither is his love only for those who love him or that are endeared to him by friendship. His love resembles the great vat of God whose works are over all His creation. It soars over all human bounds and embraces both neighbors and strangers, friends and enemies. This love is given not only to the good and gentle, but also to the disobedient, evil, and unthankful. The Christian loves every person that God has made. He loves every child of man, of whatever place or nation. His universal love does not interfere with his particular love. He continues in particular love for his relations, benefactors, friends, and country.

This love for all mankind is in itself generous and disinterested. It has no view for self-advantage and no regard for profit or praise. It disregards even the pleasure of loving. By his experience, the Christian knows that social love, if it means the love of our neighbor, is absolutely different from self-love, even of the most allowable kind. He is sure that if they are guided by God, each love will give additional force to the other until they come together, never to be divided.

This universal, disinterested love is productive of all right emotions. It produces gentleness, tenderness, sweetness, humanity, courtesy, and affability. It makes the Christian rejoice in the virtues of all people, and bear a part of their happiness. In the same manner, it helps him sympathize with their pains and have compassion for their infirmities. It creates modesty, condescension, prudence, calmness, and evenness of temper. This love is the parent of generosity, openness, and frankness—void of jealousy and suspicion. It generates candor, and willingness to believe and hope whatever is kind and friendly of every man. It also promotes an invincible patience which is never overcome by evil, but overcomes evil with good. The same love causes the Christian to converse, not only with a strict regard to truth, but with complete simplicity and genuine sincerity.

Truly, the Christian is one in whom there is no guile. He is not simply content to abstain from all expressions which are contrary to justice and truth. He tries to refrain from every unloving word, either to a present or absent person. All of his conversation is aimed either at improving himself in knowledge and virtue, or making those with whom he converses wiser, better, or happier than they were before.

This same Christian love is productive of all right actions. It leads the Christian to an earnest and steady discharge of all his social obligations. He gives his full measure to whatever relations he has. He fulfills his obligations to his friends, to his country, and to any particular community in which he is a member. Such involvement prevents willingly hurting or grieving any man. It guides him into a uniform practice of justice and mercy and requires him to do all possible good to all men. It makes him invariably committed, in every circumstance of life, to do only that to others, which, if he were in the same situation, he would want them to do to him.

As a Christian is easy on others, he is also easy on himself. He is free from pride, anger, and an impetuous and irregular self-will. He is no longer tortured by envy or malice, or with unreasonable and painful desire. He is no longer enslaved to sensual pleasures, but now has full power over both his body and his mind. He continues in a cheerful course of sobriety, temperance, and chastity. He knows how to use all things in their place and stands above low pleasures of imagination which captivate common minds. The Christian aspires to more lasting pleasures. He is never a slave to fame. Worldly acclaim does not affect him. He stands steady and collected in himself.

Because he seeks no praise, he does not fear criticism. Censure does not bother him, because he is conscious that he would not willingly offend. He knows that he has the approval of the Lord of all. Likewise, he does not fear want. He knows in whose hands the earth and its fruits rest. He knows it is impossible for God to withhold necessities from anyone who loves Him. He does not fear pain, knowing it will never be sent unless it is for his real advantage. When it is sent, he knows he will have the strength to endure it just as he has in times past. He does not fear death because he trusts God, whom he loves, with soul as well as body. He will be glad to leave the corruptible body in the dust, until it is raised incorruptible and immortal. In honor or shame, in abundance or want, in ease or in pain, in life or in death, the Christian has learned to be content and thankful in all things.

The Christian is happy in knowing there is a God. His God is an intelligent cause and Lord of all. He knows man is not a product of either blind chance or inexorable necessity. The Christian is happy in the full assurance that his God is a being of boundless wisdom. He is assured that God has the infinite power to execute all of the plans of His wisdom. He knows that God has infinite goodness, which directs all of His power to the advantage of all of His creatures. It is a continual addition to his happiness to consider God's immutable justice, all-sufficiency in himself, and complete perfection.

A further blessing warms the Christian's heart when he contemplates his existence. He looks at all the world, both visible and invisible, and he rejoices in the constant care which God takes of all of the works of His hand. In this rejoicing, he breaks out in love and praise saying, "Oh, Lord, how wonderful are your ways in the whole earth. You have set up your glory above the heavens." He sees, as it were, the Lord sitting upon His throne ruling all things well. He observes the general providence of God extended over the whole creation. He watches the effects of this providence in all things, as a joyous spectator. He sees the wisdom and goodness of God's general government applied to every particular of existence. He knows God presides over the whole universe as over a single person, watching over every person as if that person were the whole universe. He is thrilled when he reviews the various traces of God's goodness in what has happened to him throughout his own life. He knows that all of the things he has experienced have been dealt out to him by number, weight, and measure. With a triumph of soul, from observing the providence of God, the Christian sees that every action of God leads to eternity.

The Christian's particular happiness is from the clear conviction that God loves him specifically. God, the lover of his soul, is always present with him. God is never absent, even for a moment. So the Christian loves God. He feels there is none in heaven but God, none on earth whom he desires besides God. He is fully aware that God has stamped His image upon his heart. He lives only for God, only to do His will. He wants to glorify God with his body and with his spirit. He knows it will not be long before he dies, and then he shall die in the arms of God. He is excited to know that when he leaves sin and pain, he will live with God forever.

Such is the plain, unadorned picture of a true Spirit-filled Christian. Can calm reason conceive of either a more desirable or amiable character? Do you desire to be of this character? Are you conscious to yourself that you are similar to the person described here, however faintly? Do you know you ought to be such a person? Is God pleased if you are not such a person? If you are altogether such a person, you are a true Christian worthy of the name.

From this understanding of the nature of a true Christian, we can begin to consider what is genuine Christianity. It is a principle of the soul rather than a scheme or system of doctrine. In the latter sense, Christianity is a system of doctrine which describes the character of a genuine Christian. But true Christianity promises that character shall be given to anyone who will not rest until it is obtained and tells one how to obtain it.

Christianity describes Christian character in all of its parts, and in the most lively and effective manner. Points of this description are beautifully drawn in many passages of the Old Testament. These points are completed in the New Testament, retouched and finished, as the work of God. Summaries of these points may be found in the thirteenth chapter of Paul's first letter to the Corinthians and the Sermon on the Mount, which is recorded in the fifth chapter of the book of Matthew.

Christianity promises that this character can be yours and mine, if we will not rest until we obtain it. This is promised in both the Old and New Testaments. The New Testament is, in effect, all a promise. Every description of Christians in it is also a command following the general instruction: "Be imitators of me, as I am of Christ."[1] "Be imitators of those who through faith and patience inherit the promises."[2] Every command has the force of a promise. "A new heart also will I give you . . . and I will put my spirit within you, and cause you to walk in my statutes, and ye shall keep my judgments and do them."[3] "This is the covenant that I will make . . . after those days, says the Lord: I will put my laws into their minds, and write them on their hearts."[4] So, when it is said, "You shall love the Lord your God, with all of your heart, and with all of your soul, and with all of your mind,"[5] it is not only a direction of what I should do, but a promise of what God will do in me. It is exactly equivalent with what is written elsewhere: "The Lord, your God, will circumcise your heart and the heart of your offspring, so that you will love the Lord, your God, with all your heart and with all your soul."[6]

It should be observed, and does readily appear to everyone who seriously reads the New Testament, that this type of character is absolutely promised. This character is explicitly expressed under every description and command of the gospel. Christianity tells us how we may attain these promises by faith.

This faith is not merely an opinion which is no more than a form of words. Faith is not a number of opinions strung together, even if they are true. A string of opinions is no more Christian faith than a string of beads is Christian holiness.

Christian faith is not an agreement to any opinion. A person may agree to three or twenty-three creeds. He may agree to all that is written in the Bible, insofar as he understands it, yet have no Christian faith.

The Christian faith of the gospel is represented by the power wrought by God's immortal Holy Spirit in the body of man. It is the power to see into the world of spirits, into things invisible and eternal. It is the power to understand those things which are not perceived by worldly senses.

This is Christian faith as it is properly understood. It is a divine evidence or conviction given to the heart that we are reconciled to God through the work of Jesus. It is a sure confidence that we are inseparably joined to Him, our gracious reconciled Father, for all things. We are joined to Him especially for all those good things which are invisible and eternal.

How desirable is the Christian faith if only for a sense of invisible or eternal objects. All thinking and reflecting men desire a more extensive knowledge of all things invisible and eternal. They desire great certainty of these things and faculties for discerning them. Does not every thinking person want a window, an opening, which might let in light from the eternal? All are anxious because their God is so uncertain. He recognizes how little he knows about God compared to material things. He is aware he sees in a dim, sullied view. Because it is imperfect and obscure, his view of God is even more of an enigma.

True Christian faith fulfills man's desires to perceive the eternal. It gives him a more extensive knowledge of all things invisible. Living faith introduces him to what the eye has not seen, nor the ear heard, nor the heart conceived in the clearest light, with the fullest certainty and evidence. Knowing these benefits, who would not wish for such a faith? With faith comes not only this awareness, but also the fulfillment of the promise of holiness and happiness.

Christianity tells us that every Christian finds faith to be thus, and can attest to it. Through faith we are assured that these things are so. We experience them in our own hearts. What Christianity promises is accomplished in our souls. It becomes a completion of all the inward principles promised in the Gospels. It is holiness and happiness, the image of God impressed upon our spirits. It is a fountain of peace and love springing up to everlasting life.

This is the strongest evidence of true Christianity. We need not undervalue historical tradition and evidence. That evidence has its place and proper respect. But historical evidence can never replace the experiences of our own hearts. It is generally believed that historical evidence is weakened by length of time. It is said to be colored by the many hands through which it has passed over the ages. But no length of time can possibly affect this internal witness of the heart. It is as strong now, and as new, as it was 2,000 years ago. It comes now, even as in the beginning, directly from God. Time can never dry up this stream. It shall never be cut off.

Historical, traditional evidence is of an extremely complicated nature. It necessarily includes many and various considerations. Only those of strong study and understanding can be aware of its full force. On the contrary, how plain and simple is the experience of the heart. It reaches to the level of even the lowest intellectual capacity. It allows every person to say, "One thing I know: I was blind, but now I see." Living faith in the heart is an argument so plain that anyone can feel its full force.

The historical and traditional evidence of Christianity stands at a distance. Though it speaks loud and clear, it does not make such a strong impression. It gives us an account of what has occurred over the years in many distant times and places. Contrarily, the inward evidence is immediately present to all persons in all times and in all places. It is near to you. It is in your heart if you believe in the Lord Jesus Christ. In it is the evidence that God has given us eternal life. This eternal life is in His Son, Jesus.

If it were possible to remove all of the historical evidence of Christianity, the Christian with this internal evidence would stand firm and unshaken. He could say to all those around him, "You cannot hurt my evidence of Christianity. You can no more hurt it than the tyrants could hurt the spirits of the martyrs."

At times, it appears that God has allowed the external evidence of Christianity to become dimmed and encumbered for this very purpose. It was done so Christians might not rely upon it. They are required to look into themselves. They must attest to the light shining in their hearts.

It seems as if God has allowed all sorts of objections to be raised against the traditional historical evidence of

Christianity in this age. Men of learning and wisdom are unwilling to give it up. They continue to defend this evidence. Not being able to rest their whole argument upon it, they must seek a deeper and firmer support of their faith. Without the internal evidence of a living faith, they cannot long support their cause. If they do not gain the internal evidence of a living faith, they will lose the battle. In a short time, those whom they wish to convince will be lost to deism.

Many of those who call themselves Christians have neither Christian faith nor love. They have no internal evidence of a living faith. They have not entered into this relationship through the blood atonement of Jesus. They do not love God with all their hearts. They do not love their neighbor as themselves. They have not learned to be content in every state of their life. They cannot give thanks, even in want, pain, and death. They are not holy in heart—superior to pride, anger, and foolish desires. Neither are they holy in life. They do not walk as Christ walked. Most contemporary Christianity centers upon opinions, with a few outward observances. Many agnostics reflect greater morality and honesty than these self-styled Christians.

Nominal Christians need to be shamed out of the poor superstition which they call Christianity. Reason can be used to laugh them out of their dead Christianity and empty forms—void of Spirit, faith, or love. Reason should convince them that religious pageantry, if there is nothing in the heart corresponding with the outward show, is absolutely unworthy of God. Even men with average understanding can show them that while they are attempting to please God through rituals, they are only beating the air. The agnostics will press on, pushing their victories, until they have conquered all those who do not know God. Then, God whom they do not know, will rise up in His mighty love, and conquer the hearts of all doubters.

Oh, how real Christians wish that time were now. How they long for everyone to participate in that great and precious inward living faith. How true Christians are pained when they hear others using silly terms of Christianity which they have been taught. They call the Holy Spirit, with His deepest wisdom and highest happiness, fanaticism. Such ignorance would be despicable in any eyes but those of the true Christian. The true Christian despises no one. He loves the doubter as he loves his own soul. He would lay down his life for every man's sake.

Some will have the honest objection that internal Christianity affects only those who receive it. There is truth in that objection. It does primarily affect those who receive it. However, it does not affect them only. In the nature of things, it is not as strong an evidence to others as it is to them. Yet it may bring a degree of evidence and reflect some truth to others. There are several reasons for this. First, you can see the beauty and loveliness of true Christianity when it is properly understood. There is nothing to be desired in comparison with it. The Scripture promises this and says it may be obtained by faith and no other way. Next, one should be able to clearly see how desirable Christian faith is on account of its own intrinsic value. Holiness and happiness can be obtained in no other way. The more you work to attain virtue and happiness, the more you become convinced that they cannot be attained except by Christian faith. Your personal experience is evidence enough; you need not look to other men for this evidence. Finally, can you have any assurance that you can obtain any of these virtues of Christianity if you do not have an inward experience of living faith?

Now we can look to others with this living faith for useful internal evidence. There were those who were miserable, but now are happy. That is a very strong evidence of the truth of Christianity. Until this is experienced by an individual, the experience of others is as strong an evidence as may be afforded. Rely upon what you see occurring in the lives of others as your evidence, and not upon the opinions which they might hold. Never miss this point. What the Scripture promises, true Christians have and enjoy. All can see what living faith has done and acknowledge it is of God. The God of power and love can make all of us Christians with living faith, as He has throughout the ages.

From "Letter to Dr. Conyers Middleton," January 4, 1749.

Epilogue

Scriptural Christianity, as we have seen, is to be filled with the Holy Spirit.[1] Have you received the Holy Spirit? If you have not, you are not yet a Christian. A Christian is one who is anointed with the Holy Spirit and with power.[2] He is a Christian who has received this Holy Spirit from Christ. He is not a Christian who has not received Him. It is not possible to have received the Holy Spirit and not know it.[3]

I believe every person who has not yet received Him should pray for the witness of God's Spirit with his spirit that he is a child of God. Everyone who desires this grace of God is to wait for it and to seek it in prayer. This is the express direction of Jesus, himself. In the Sermon on the Mount, He says, "Ask, and it will be given to you; seek, and you will find; knock, and it will be opened you . . . For every one who asks receives, and he who seeks finds, and to him who knocks it will be opened."[4] Here we are in the plainest manner directed to ask as a means of receiving. We are to seek to find the grace of God, the pearl of great price. We are to knock, to continue asking and seeking, if we would receive the Holy Spirit and enter into God's kingdom.[5] That there might be no doubt, Jesus labors this point in a more particular way. He appeals to every man's own heart. "What man of you, if his son asks him for bread, will give him a stone? Or if he asks for a fish, will give him a serpent? If you then, who are evil, know how to give good gifts to your children, how much more will your Father who is in heaven give good things to those who ask him!"[6] Or, as Jesus said on another occasion, "How much more will the heavenly Father give the Holy Spirit to those who ask him!" It should be particularly observed, that the persons directed to ask had not yet received the Holy Spirit. Jesus directs them to pray for the Holy Spirit and promises that their prayers will be heard. Upon asking, they would receive the Holy Spirit from Him whose mercy is over all His works.[8] From this Scripture we must infer all who desire this grace of God are to wait for it in prayer.[9]

Pray to Him day and night, until you know you believe in Jesus and can say, "My Lord and my God," by the power of the Holy Spirit. Remember to pray always. Do not quit, until you can lift up your hands to heaven and declare to Him who lives forever, "Lord, you know all things. You know I love you."[10]

May we all then experience what it is to be altogether Christians. May we all be saved freely by His grace, through the redemption that is in Jesus. May we all experience peace with God through Jesus Christ, rejoicing in the hope of the glory of God. May we all have the love of God shed abroad in our hearts by the Holy Spirit given to us.[11]

Footnotes and Scripture References

Footnotes to Prologue
1. Eph. 5:14.
2. Ezek. 36:27.
3. Isa. 44:3.
4. John 14:20.
5. John 14:17.
6. The word "fanatics" has been substituted for the Wesleyan expression, "enthusiasts." The meanings are synonymous, with enthusiasts being outdated. The same substitution has been made elsewhere for the word "enthusiasts" or "enthusiasm."
7. Matt. 5:13.

Chapter 1
1. Nehemiah Curnock, ed., *The Journal of the Rev. John Wesley*, (London: Charles H. Kelly, 1909), February 1, 1738, entry.
2. "Wesley," Encyclopedia Britannica, 1960 ed., vol. 23, pp. 515-516.
3. "Circumcision of the Heart, Standard Sermon XIII," preached at St. Mary's Church, Oxford, England, January 1, 1733.
4. *The Journal of the Rev. John Wesley*, February 1, 1738.
5. Ibid.
6. Ibid., October 17, 1735.
7. Ibid., January 23-25, 1736.
8. Ibid., February 24, 1736.
9. Ibid., June 22, 1736.
10. Ibid., December 27, 1737.
11. Ibid., January 9, 1738.
12. Ibid., January 24, 1738.
13. Ibid., January 29, 1738.
14. Ibid.
15. Phil. 3:9.
16. *The Journal of the Rev. John Wesley*, February 3, 1738.
17. Ibid., February 7, 1738.
18. Ibid., February 18, 1738.
19. Ibid., February 28, 1738.
20. Ibid., March 23, 1738.
21. Ibid., March 26, 1738.
22. Ibid., March 27, 1738.
23. Ibid., April 22, 1738.
24. Ibid., May 1, 1738.
25. Ibid., May 3, 1738.
26. Ibid., May 19, 1738.
27. Ibid., May 24, 1738, items 13, 14.

28. Ibid., May 25, 1738.
29. Ibid., May 28, 1738.
30. Ibid., July 2, 1738.
31. Ibid., July 6, 1738.
32. Ibid., August 8, 1738.
33. Ibid., September 17, 1738.
34. Ibid., December 5, 1738.
35. Ibid., January 1, 1739.
36. Ibid., March 2, 1739.
37. Ibid., March 8, 1739.
38. Ibid., April 17, 1739.
39. Ibid., April 21, 1739.
40. Ibid., April 26, 1739.
41. Ibid., April 27, 1739.
42. Ibid., April 30, 1739.
43. Ibid., May 1, 1739.
44. Ibid., August 21, 1744.
45. Introduction, *Forty-Four Sermons*, par. 1.

Chapter 2
1. Rom. 14:17, KJV.
2. Acts 21:20.
3. Acts 15:1, KJV.
4. Mark 12:30.
5. Ps. 18:1, 2.
6. Ps. 32:1.
7. Charles Wesley, "Sons of God, Triumphant Rise," *Hymns and Sacred Poems* (1739), From *The Poetical Works of John and Charles Wesley*, collected by G. Osborn (London: Wesleyan-Methodist Conference, 1868), vol. 1, p. 170.
8. 1 John 5:11, 12.
9. John 17:3.
10. Matt. 28:20
11. Rom. 6:23.
12. John 3:16.
13. Isa. 53:5; 1 Pet. 2:24

Chapter 3
1. Matt. 7:12.
2. Horace, Ep. 1, xvi, 52.
3. Matt. 22:37.
4. Matt. 22:39.
5. 1 John 5:1.
6. John 1:12, KJV.

7. 1 John 5:4, KJV.
8. John 3:36, John 5:24.
9. Life of Johnson II xi.

Chapter 4
1. Gen. 1:26, 27
2. Eph. 4:24.
3. 1 John 4:8.
4. Gen. 1:31.
5. Ibid., 2:17
6. Ibid., 3:10
7. John 3:8
8. Ibid.
9. Ibid., 3:9
10. Eph. 1:18
11. Matt. 9:2.
12. John 8:11, KJV
13. Eph. 4:15.

Chapter 5
1. Gal. 3:26, KJV.
2. John 1:12, 13, KJV.
3. 1 John 5:1, KJV.
4. Rom. 6:2.
5. 1 John 3:1, 2, KJV
6. Ibid., 3:9, KJV.
7. Ibid., 3:5.
8. Ibid., 3:6.
9. Ibid., 3:7-10.
10. Ibid., 5:18.
11. Rom. 5:1.
12. John 14:27.
13. Ibid., 16:33, KJV.
14. 1 Pet. 1:3.
15. Rom. 8:14-16.
16. Matt. 5:4.
17. John 16:22.
18. Rom. 5:2, KJV.
19. 1 Pet. 1:5, ff.
20. Rev. 21:3, 4, KJV.
21. Rom. 5:5.
22. Gal. 4:6.
23. 1 John 5:15.
24. Ibid., 5:1.

25. Song of Sol. 2:16.
26. Ps. 45:2.
27. 1 John 3:14.
28. Ibid., 4:7.
29. Ibid., 5:3.

Chapter 6
1. 1 Cor. 2:12.
2. 2 Cor. 1:12.
3. Gal. 5:19.
4. Ibid., 5:16, 17.
5. 1 John 3:9.
6. Gal. 5:18.
7. 1 Tim. 1:8,9,11.
8. 1 Cor. 3:1.
9. 1 John 3:24.
10. Isa. 12:2.

Chapter 7
1. Mark 16:17, 18, KJV.
2. Acts 2:16, 17, KJV.
3. 1 Cor. 12:4-11, KJV.
4. Jerome, ca. 340-420, was an historian and the translator of the Vulgate Bible. He finally headquartered in Palestine from 386 until his death. As an historian, he continued work on Eusebius's *Chronicle*, the first post-apostolic Church history.
5. Chrysostom, John, ca. 345-407, became Bishop of Constantinople, ca. 398. He was famous for great preaching while at Antioch, ca. 386-398.
6. Augustine, Bishop of Hippo in North Africa, ca. 392, wrote contrary to Chrysostom. In his famous *City of God*, (ca. 412), Section XXII:8 was on miracles. That title was, "Of miracles which were wrought that the world might believe in Christ, and which have not ceased since the world believed." In that essay, Augustine listed a variety of miracles, including healings and six raisings from the dead as having occurred in his diocese at Hippo.
7. John Wesley did not state that miracles completely ceased. He had seen too many in his own ministry to ever affirm such. His statement is that, "very few instances were to be found after then."
8. John Wesley, "The More Excellent Way," Thomas Jackson, ed., *The Works of John Wesley*, (London: Wesleyan Conference, 1872), vol. 7, Sermon LXXXIX, pp. 26-27.
9. *The Journal of the Rev. John Wesley*, August 15, 1750.
10. Justin Martyr was born in Samaria and died a martyr's death in Rome, ca. 165. He wrote two defenses of Christianity, "Apology," ca. 153,

and "Dialogue with Trypho," a little later.

11. Irenaeus, ca. 115-200, became Bishop of Lyons, ca. 175. He wrote "Against Heresies," ca. 185. He was raised in Smyrna and there was exposed to Polycarp, whose ministry began before 110.

12. Theophilus, Bishop of Antioch, a contemporary with Irenaeus and a successor to Ignatius.

13. Tertullian, ca. 150-225, became a follower of Montanism. Known as the father of Latin theology, he ably defended Christianity in several writings.

14. Minutius Felix, Marcus, ca. 200, was the first Latin apologist. He wrote dialogue to "Octavius."

15. Origen, ca. 182-251, a pupil of Clement and ordained presbyter in Caesarea. Origen completed several writings including, "Hexapla," De Principiis," and "Against Celsus."

16. Cyprian, ca. 200-258, became Bishop of Carthage, ca. 250. Influenced by Tertullian, he left several writings.

17. Arnobius, ob. ca. 330, was a Christian apologist in the time of Diocletian (284-305). He had Lactantius as a pupil.

18. Lactantius, ob. ca. 330, was converted ca. 301. He became an advisor of Constantine and tutor of his son, Crispus. His "Institutione Divinae," was an exposition and defense of the Christian faith.

19. Compare with Acts 9:36 43.

20. Raisings from the dead are not uncommon in Christian history. Wesley reported that Thomas Merick came back to life after prayer by Wesley and several others, *Journal*, December 23, 1742.

Other accounts of raisings may be read in St. Teresa, *The Life of St. Teresa* (Westminster: The Newman Press 1962), p. 288, and Alvar Munez Cabeza de Vaca, *The Narrative of Alvar Munez Cabeza de Vaca* (Barre, Massachusetts: The Imprint Society 1972), pp. 88, 89.

DeVaca was a Spanish explorer who developed a miracle ministry among the Texas Indians, 1528. St. Teresa was a Spanish nun, ca. 1515-1582. Also see Augustine (supra footnote 6).

In our time, scientific reports of the raising of the dead have put the phenomena beyond question.

21. James 5:13-15.

22. John 9.

23. Acts 2:17.

24. 1 Cor. 12:29, 30.

25. There are several expressions of the gift of tongues. One is speaking in unknown languages to spread the gospel. Another is a spiritual singing or praying known as "jubilation."

A detailed account of speaking in previously unknown languages for spreading the gospel is in the Cabeza de Vaca narrative, (supra footnote 20). He reported, "We came across a great variety and number of languages, and God our Lord favored us with a knowledge of all, because they always could understand us and we understood them . . . although we spoke six languages, not everywhere could we use them, since we found more than a thousand different ones" (pp. 129, 130).

Speaking in tongues as a spiritual experience of "jubilation," or "jubilus," has been known in the church from the earliest times. Augustine mentioned it more than twenty times in his writings and called it miraculous. Chrysostom also recorded it, as did Jerome. Eddie Ensley, "Where Has All the Jubilation Gone?" *New Covenant*, vol. 6 no. 7, January 1977, p. 18ff.

In early Methodism, jubilation was reported by Thomas Walsh in his journal entry of March 8, 1751. He wrote, "This morning the Lord gave me a language that I knew not of, raising my soul to Him in a wonderful manner." Thomas Jackson, ed., *The Lives of Early Methodist Preachers*, 4th ed., (London: Wesleyan Conference, 1865), vol. 3, p. 211.

One well-known historian affirmed different types of tongue speaking by writing, "Certainly the conception of a proclamation of the Gospel in many foreign languages is inconsistent with what we know of speaking with tongues elsewhere," (1 Cor. 14:2-9), Williston Walker, *The History of the Christian Church*, (New York: Charles Scribner's Sons, 1959) p. 21.

26. An excellent review of the history of tongues is Kelsey's *Tongue Speaking*. The details of the Huguenot outbreak of the charismata are included in it, pp. 52ff, Morton T. Kelsey, *Tongue Speaking*, (Garden City, New York: Waymark Books/Doubleday & Company, Inc., 1968).

27. 1 Cor. 12:11, KJV.

Chapter 8

1. "Enthusiasts."
2. Rom. 8:15, 16.
3. 1 Cor. 14:20.
4. Rom. 8:14.
5. 1 John 2:3, 5, 29.
6. Ibid., 3:14, 19.
7. Ibid., 4:13.
8. Ibid., 3:24.
9. Ibid., 4:19, KJV.
10. 1 Cor. 2:12, KJV.
11. 2 Cor. 1:12, KJV.
12. John 3:8.
13. Matt. 3:2.
14. Mark 1:15.
15. Acts 2:38, KJV.
16. Ibid., 3:19, KJV.
17. Eph. 2:1, 2, 5, 6.

18. 1 John 5:3.
19. John 14:21.
20. 1 Cor. 2:14.

Chapter 9
1. John 8:12.
2. Phil. 4:4.
3. Rom. 2:14, 15.
4. 2 Tim. 3:16.
5. Acts 23:1.
6. Ibid., 24:16.
7. Gal. 2:20.
8. Heb. 8:10.
9. Matt. 6:22, KJV.
10. Phil. 3:7, 8, KJV.
11. Tenth verse of "Watch In All Things," from *Hymns and Sacred Poems*, 1742.

Chapter 10
1. Phil. 4:7.
2. Eccles. 9:4.

Chapter 11
1. Matt. 5:48, KJV.
2. Phil. 3:12, 15, KJV.
3. 1 John 2:20, KJV.
4. Matt. 24:36.
5. 1 John 2:26.
6. Ibid., 3:7.
7. Ibid., 2:12-14.
8. Rom. 6:1, 2.
9. Ibid., 6:6, 7.
10. Ibid., 6:14, 18.
11. 1 Pet. 4:1, 2.
12. 1 John 3:8, 9.
13. Ibid., 5:18.
14. 1 Pet. 1:9, 10.
15. Ibid., 1:12.
16. 1 John 1:8.
17. Ibid., 1:10.
18. Ibid., 3:7, 8, 10.

19. Luke 6:40.
20. 2 Cor. 10:4; 2 Cor. 10:4, KJV.
21. Matt. 10:24, 25.
22. Gal. 2:20, KJV.
23. 1 John 3:3.
24. Mark 3:5.
25. 1 John 4:17 KJV.
26. Ibid., 1:5, 7
27. Ibid., 1:9.
28. Deut. 30:6.
29. Ezek. 36:25 ff.

Chapter 12
1. Acts 2:1-4, KJV.
2. 1 Cor. 12:28-30.
3. Gal. 5:22-24.
4. 1 Thess. 1:3.
5. Heb. 11:1.
6. Rom. 8:15.
7. 1 Cor. 12:3.
8. Rom. 8:16.
9. Gal. 2:20.
10. Rom. 5:1.
11. Phil. 1:23.
12. Heb. 2:15.
13. Rom. 5:5.
14. Gal. 4:6.
15. 1 John 5:10.
16. Ibid., 4:11.
17. Ps. 145:9.
18. 1 Cor. 13:4.
19. Matt. 25:40, KJV.
20. Acts 2:44, 45.
21. Matt. 5:16.
22. 1 Pet. 2:25.
23. Acts 17:31.
24. Heb. 12:14.
25. John 7:7.
26. Acts 19:25-27.
27. Ibid., 24:5.
28. Ibid., 21:28.
29. Heb. 11:35-37.
30. Matt. 16:18.

31. Isa. 2:2,4.
32. Ibid., 11:10-12.
33. Ibid., 11:6,9.
34. Rom. 11:1,11,12,25,26, KJV.
35. Ps. 144:15.
36. Isa. 60:1.
37. Ibid., 60:16-19,21.
38. 1 Tim. 4:12.

Chapter 13
1. 1 Cor. 11:1.
2. Heb. 6:12.
3. Ezek. 36:26,27, KJV.
4. Heb. 8:10.
5. Matt. 22:37.
6. Deut. 30:6.

Epilogue
1. "Scriptural Christianity," *Forty-Four Sermons*, Sermon IV.
2. "Awake, Thou That Sleepest," *Forty-Four Sermons*, Sermon III, part II, p. 10.
3. Ibid., part IV, p. 9.
4. Matt. 7:7,8.
5. "The Means of Grace," *Forty-Four Sermons*, Sermon XII, part III, p. 1.
6. Matt. 7:9-11.
7. Luke 11:13.
8. "The Means of Grace," part III, p. 2.
9. Ibid., p. 6.
10. "The Almost Christian," *Forty-Four Sermons*, Sermon II, part III, p. 10.
11. Ibid., p. 11.